GW00375018

ALWAYS TRYING

ALWAYS TRYING

MARK JOHNSTON

A TRAINER'S YEAR

John Scanlon

with a foreword by Paul Haigh

Printers & Publishers

Published by Portway Press Limited

First published in 2000
by Portway Press Limited
Halifax West Yorkshire HX1 1XE
Tel: 01422 330330 Fax: 01422 398017
E-mail: timeform@timeform.com
Internet: www.timeform.com

© John Scanlon

All rights reserved.
No part of this publication may be reproduced,
stored in a retrieval system, or transmitted
in any form or by any means, electronic, mechanical,
photocopying, recording or otherwise,
without the prior permission of the copyright holders.

ISBN 1 901570 14 2

Printed and bound by
the Charlesworth Group,
Huddersfield, UK. 01484 517077

ALWAYS TRYING

Dedication

This book is dedicated to the memory of my parents, John and Cathie Scanlon, who both died in 1999.

They might not have appreciated the content, but I hope they would have approved of the effort invested in the work and the love with which it is dedicated to them.

ALWAYS TRYING

Author's Acknowledgements

T his book would simply not have been possible without the assistance, support and understanding of a whole range of people, not least the staff of Mark Johnston Racing Limited. Every request for assistance or information was answered positively, efficiently and courteously and I extend sincere thanks to Debbie Albion and the girls in the Administration Office, Mikaelle Lebreton, Philip Marrison and all the staff for their help and encouragement.

Thanks are also due to those of Mark's owners whom I met during the year for their tolerance and understanding in allowing me to share vicariously in their racecourse experiences and, in some cases, their hospitality.

I would also wish to express my gratitude to Paul Haigh for agreeing to write the foreword, and to Jim McGrath, Nigel Townsend and all at Portway Press for their patience in guiding me through the project to the bitter end!

I am also grateful to Alan Byrne, editor of the *Racing Post*, for permission to reproduce extracts from articles (mostly by Mark Johnston) which appeared in that newspaper during the year.

To Mark and Deirdre Johnston and the boys I offer my profound thanks for allowing me into their home and into the heart of their business to enjoy and endure with them the peaks and troughs of their racing year and to record those experiences publicly. I am grateful to them for the warmth of their welcome and the extent of their hospitality, for their endless enthusiasm and practical assistance and most of all for their patience. I thank Mark in particular for his honesty and his trust.

No words are adequate to express my debt of thanks to my wife, Mairi, and to my children, Michael and Clare, for all their support, encouragement, enthusiasm, assistance, belief, patience and, above all, love without which I would simply not have been able to complete this project.

March 2000

Picture Acknowledgements

Grateful acknowledgement is made to the following for permission to reproduce their copyright photographs and works:

Ed Byrne

Emirates Racing Association

John Grossick

Tim Hetherington/Musto Ltd

Alec Russell

George Selwyn

Foreword
by Paul Haigh

Trying to write objectively about a colleague is always a tricky business. Gush too much, and people say you're crawling. Criticise him, even constructively, and it's even money he'll never speak to you again.

Fortunately Mark Johnston makes life fairly easy in this respect because all you need to do is list those fields in which he is more than just competent to realise the man is a bit of a bloody polymath.

A qualified vet, an efficient businessman, a quite irritating demonstrator of how easy it is to write a column in the *Racing Post*, he is primarily a racehorse trainer who, simply through his own ability and hard work, has established himself firmly in the top flight at home and as someone whose horses have to be reckoned with wherever they run in the world.

No race is too small for Johnston to want to win it, and no race is so big or so distant that he will duck having a tilt at it as long as he can feel confident of going there with a realistic chance. One thing you always know about Mark's horses is that every single animal that leaves his yard is being sent out to win—hence the title of this book—as his thoroughly delightful wife Deirdre once told me sternly when I made a casual inquiry as to whether one of theirs was running...well, you know, just for the sake of it.

If you campaign horses as openly and honestly as the Johnstons do, then you inevitably suffer some disappointments. Happily, however, you have plenty of triumphs to go with them.

In this his first book, lawyer-turned-academic-turned-racing writer John Scanlon has chronicled one year in the life of perhaps the busiest and most interesting stable around.

John is a true racing fan whose enthusiasm radiates in everything he writes. He has gone to the trouble of getting inside the day to day workings of the yard that has regenerated the historic training centre of Middleham, describing its tribulations and delights, as well as the fortunes of its horses—from maidens on the all-weather to Group 1 performers in the USA and the Far East—in a way that guarantees fascinating reading for anyone who's intrigued by what is both the simplest and the most complex sport on earth.

ALWAYS TRYING

Contents

ALWAYS TRYING

Introduction

S hortly after 8 am on Tuesday May 4th 1999. Mark Johnston and I make our way across Middleham's Low Moor through early-morning fog to the seven-furlong all-weather gallop, to join second lot preparing for exercise. In truth, such is the blanket enveloping these historic training grounds that it would have come as no great surprise to the writer had the first figures to emerge from the eerie stillness been equine phantoms of Middleham's rich history. Perhaps a charger bearing Richard of York, venturing forth from his stronghold of Middleham Castle during the Wars of the Roses, or even locally-trained Classic winners of the past, such as The Flying Dutchman, Apology and Dante.

Eventually the string comes into view. As it canters past I ask Mark whether foggy conditions are a particular hindrance to the morning's work. Leaving aside a dangerous mix of poor visibility and speed, he comments that there is actually one advantage, in that they enable him to hear the horses before he can see them, allowing breathing problems to be identified more easily. On reaching the bottom of the gallop the horses circle at a walk, their riders reporting any problems. A three-year-old colt called High Regard has apparently coughed several times since leaving his box, so his lass is told to walk him home. Before we go any further Johnston phones his office with an instruction to scratch the horse from its immediate racing engagements. Those on horses earmarked for fast work are now given instructions, after which Mark and I make our way to the all-weather strip to observe work at close quarters. By this stage Johnston has already supervised first lot, dealt with queries in the administration office, taken the first few of a deluge of calls on his mobile phone, and scrutinised the five-day entries in the *Racing Post*. He has also chaired, fairly aggressively, the stable's weekly management breakfast meeting. Back at base his administration manager Debbie Albion and her staff are already acting upon a number of the issues raised shortly after 7am! We now watch some encouraging work, notably by a two-year-old filly called Kashra, who goes well in the hands of senior work rider Bobby Elliott.

This is a day full of optimism. Later on Doonaree, a three-year-old colt by top sire Sadler's Wells, unraced as a juvenile, but now the winner of races at Catterick and Newcastle in impressive fashion, runs in the Victor Chandler Chester Vase, a Group 3 race and an established Derby trial. He's the likely favourite and Johnston exudes quiet confidence as to his prospects. Additionally, Kashra holds an entry for a median auction race at Hamilton on Thursday. On the evidence of the work we've just seen, she has it at her mercy.

After third lot, we set off for Chester. The journey provides an opportunity for Mark and his wife, Deirdre, to deal with calls. For example, they finalise jockey arrangements, liaise with owners, discuss travel plans and so forth. I'm impressed with their easy manner and obvious enthusiasm. Unlike many within racing they are happy to co-operate with the press, both appreciating the value of publicity, for the benefit of Mark Johnston Racing Limited and also for the greater good of the sport. Deirdre finalises details of an appearance on the Racing Channel scheduled for the following day, when Etterby Park is set to run in the Chester Cup. We discuss why Doonaree has been entered in the Chester Vase as opposed to any of the other Classic trials. Mark points out that whilst full of potential Doonaree requires to demonstrate his ability in listed or Group company before Classic plans can realistically be considered. I wonder why the horse has been entered at Chester, a turning left-handed circuit, when his main target is the Budweiser Irish Derby on the right-handed, galloping, wide-open expanse of the Curragh. Mark points out that since Doonaree was able to handle Catterick then Chester should be within his compass.

As we near Chester, Deirdre spies a McDonald's (a secret passion of hers!) and we stop for lunch. Any preconceived ideas I had about the champagne and caviar lifestyle of a top trainer disappear as we tuck into quarter-pounders and chips! Suitably fortified, we move on to Chester. Unusually, this is a day when the Johnstons do not have to look after an owner, as Doonaree's lives abroad and his racing manager is also away. It's a pleasantly warm afternoon and a large crowd creates that special atmosphere which always seems to imbue the May meeting on the Roodeye. Beforehand conversation is relaxed, but there's no doubting the growing feeling of excitement as post time approaches. Looking at the racecard one can't help but be impressed by the quality of past winners of the Vase. Hot Grove in 1977; Henbit, Shergar and Old Vic in the 'eighties, and Toulon, Armiger and Luso in the 'nineties. Mark muses upon the conditions of the race which state that a "trophy value £650" is included in the value of the prize for the winning owner. Such practice has recently been the the subject of unfavourable comment from Paul Haigh in his column in the *Racing Post.* Deirdre contrasts these arrangements with her experiences abroad, particularly in Dubai, where valuable trophies are given in addition to prize money. However, we all know that prize money, whether inclusive of a trophy or not, is not the principal aim of those with runners in the Vase today: keeping that Classic dream alive is the main object of the exercise.

Whilst Mark saddles, Deirdre explains that though Doonaree did not run as a two-year-old, a glimpse of his potential was seen in one sparkling piece of work; thus his development into Classic hopeful has not been entirely unexpected. Darryll Holland arrives in the paddock a little late, adjusting his gloves (right and left-handed white Footjoy golf gloves) as he chats briefly to Mark and Deirdre. Perhaps unusually, it is not Johnston's policy to give 'instructions' to his jockeys. Equally, one can be certain Holland knows what is expected of him. It becomes obvious that Doonaree has indeed been installed as favourite; nonetheless, our confidence is overtaken by nerves and anxiety as the horse goes to post. Keeping everything crossed, we make our way to the owners and trainers viewing area. Will Doonaree impress, as he had in his previous races? Is he the horse most likely to deliver a Group 1 success to Kingsley House this season? Darryll settles him on the outside of the small field and, passing the winning post with one circuit left, Doonaree is going particularly well. However, five furlongs from home we see altogether too much activity on the part of Holland and it quickly becomes clear that this won't be Doonaree's day. He struggles around the home bend and finishes last.

The run appears too bad to be true. On dismounting Holland tells Mark that the horse "was making a noise". I'm immediately reminded of our conversation on the Low Moor this morning and struck by its irony. Clearly disappointed, Mark heads to the weighing room to enquire about the possibility of having the horse scoped. Incredibly, no facilities are available on course, though officials suggest that Doonaree could be taken to Liverpool Vet School. The disappointment and feeling of anticlimax is almost tangible and Mark is frustrated by his inability to investigate the cause of the problem immediately. From his mobile phone he calls the offices of the National Trainers' Federation to complain about the lack of facilities for endoscopy at Chester.

Whilst making our way back to the car Mark receives a call from Robynne Watton, the travelling head lass, who is unhappy about Doonaree's condition. She asks Mark to call at the racecourse stables. Upon inspection, and despite not having had a hard race, Mark agrees with her that the horse seems distressed and wonders whether its condition is consistent with some wind or heart problem. However, he realises that it is far too early to reach any conclusions and eventually decides to scope the horse at home after morning exercise. He feels too much is made of horses 'making a noise' in races, knowing that this sometimes occurs because they have come under increased pressure. Conscious of Instruction H14 laid down by the Jockey Club, requiring trainers to report anything which might have adversely affected the performance of any horse they train, he decides it would be irresponsible of him to make any diagnosis without further examination.

The journey homeward is subdued and Johnston's mood sombre. Doonaree's credentials as a potential Group 1 winner have not, for whatever reason, withstood their first serious examination. To make matters worse, news comes through from Kingsley House that the computer software package used to deal with the stable's entries has failed; furthermore, the consultant cannot be reached. Numerous phone calls are made in an effort to obtain assistance in accessing the programme, but when we arrive at the yard shortly after 6 pm the problem has still not been resolved. The prospect of dealing with the entries manually for a stable of over 150 inmates does little to cheer Johnston, and when Susanna Ballinger, resident vet and assistant trainer, pops her head round the door to report that, amongst other things, Kashra is lame, the day seems complete. However, Mark Johnston is made of stern stuff. The fierce determination and enthusiasm which has driven his yard to join the best around (in terms of races won Johnston is the leading trainer in Britain) is quickly evident in his resolve to put the disappointments of such a day behind him and to kick on towards other clearly defined goals.

The main body of this book charts how Johnston and his team responded to such challenges in 1999. But first, let me introduce you to Middleham and to the man, horses and staff who have done so much to restore it as a premier training centre.

CHAPTER ONE

Middleham

There is a special atmosphere about the historic Yorkshire town of Middleham which even the most casual of visitors could not fail to sense. Twinned with Agincourt and dominated by Middleham Castle, the town is steeped in the turbulent history of the north of England.

Set in the Yorkshire Dales between Wensleydale and Coverdale, the Domesday Book records the existence of Middleham by reference to the landmark William's Hill, the site of the first castle at Middleham around 1086. This site was abandoned in the twelfth century in favour of the location of the present castle, the focal point of which is its great stone keep, thought to have been constructed by Robert Fitzranulph around 1170. In 1270 Middleham passed into the ownership of the powerful Nevill family and remained under their control until the death of Richard Nevill, Earl of Warwick ('the Kingmaker') at the Battle of Barnet in April 1471. The following year, Edward IV's brother, Richard, Duke of Gloucester, was granted Warwick's estates north of the Trent, including Middleham. Later that year Richard married Ann Nevill, Warwick's younger daughter. Richard had spent most of his formative years at Middleham Castle under Warwick's care and his union with Nevill helped him to attract a large following from Middleham and the surrounding area. It was at Middleham that Richard plotted to seize the crown following his brother's death early in 1483. Having arranged for the imprisonment of Edward's sons and rightful heirs in the Tower of London, Richard assumed the throne and was crowned Richard III at Westminster on July 6th 1483.

However, Richard's reign was brief, unpopular and marred by personal tragedy. His only son, Edward of Middleham, who had been born at the castle, died there after a short illness in April 1484, aged 10. Fuelled by speculation as to the fate of the princes in the Tower and Richard's responsibility for their disappearance, the House of Lancaster mounted a further challenge to the crown through Henry Tudor, Earl of Richmond. The day of reckoning arrived on August 22nd 1485 at Bosworth Field in Leicestershire. Richard's army, including many men of Middleham and Richmondshire, was overwhelmed and he was killed in battle. Henry Tudor was crowned Henry VII there and then on the battlefield. Middleham and its estates were seized by Henry and from that moment on Middleham's pivotal role in the history of the north began to decline.

Shakespeare memorably recorded the stricken Richard's plight in the heat of battle with the famous entreaty: "A horse! A horse! My kingdom for a horse!" (*King Richard III*, Act V, Scene iii). How unfortunate for Richard that he had not been able to manipulate the campaign so as to lure the Lancastrian forces to Middleham! His cries for a horse would surely have been answered there. In the twelfth century a French Cistercian Order of Monks established Jervaulx Abbey, just two miles south of Middleham, where they were instrumental in introducing the practice of breeding horses to the area. Whilst their work was restricted to breeding and training Dales horses, this set the pattern for Middleham's involvement in the horse industry over the centuries. Following the establishment of the thoroughbred in England, Middleham became a magnet, as the natural training grounds of the High and Low Moors provided the perfect environment for conditioning racehorses. Professional trainers were recorded in Middleham as early as 1765 when Isaac Cape, a former jockey, established himself at Tupgill. By 1739 the town had a racecourse of its own on High Moor, and as horses could be walked to local courses such as Richmond, Ripon, Catterick and Northallerton, Middleham soon became firmly established as a premier centre for training racehorses. The possibility that its training grounds, especially the High Moor, might also have the advantage of bestowing a benefit similar to 'altitude training' has been considered recently. While this theory is not entirely discounted by Johnston, he remains to be convinced of its merit.

Throughout the eighteenth and nineteenth centuries many great horses were trained at Middleham and success in the Classics was commonplace. Indeed, in 1822 James Croft, Master of Glasgow House, trained the first, second, third and fourth in the St Leger. Into the twentieth century Middleham continued to be at the forefront of the British racing industry, principally through the efforts of the Peacock family. In 1932 Dobson Peacock became the first Middleham trainer to saddle 100 winners in a season, a considerable feat when one considers the comparative disadvantage which he would have suffered at that time in travelling his horses. After relinquishing control of the historic Manor House stables (now home to James Bethell's string) to his son, Matt, in 1935 the family's enviable record was soon enhanced even further by success in the Derby. Despite an increasing influence of Newmarket on the racing scene in general and the Classics in particular, Matt Peacock trained more winners than anyone else in Britain between 1936 and 1939. Six years later his success in the Derby with Dante sparked celebrations in the town reputed to have lasted for weeks. Tragically, Dante never ran again, a progressively deteriorating eye condition known as Periodic Opthalmia, or moonblindness, afflicting him to such an extent that by St Leger time he was virtually blind in both eyes.

In the post-war period, success for Middleham was achieved mainly by Captain Neville Crump under National Hunt Rules. No fewer than three

Grand National winners, five Scottish Grand National winners and two Welsh Grand National winners were sent out by him from Warwick House, now Mark Johnston's second yard and home to his army of two-year-olds. Crump was champion trainer in 1951/2 and again in 1956/7 but success at the very highest level on the Flat eluded Middleham's trainers from Dante's Derby until the arrival in the town of Mark and Deirdre Johnston late in 1988, when they purchased Kingsley House stables, which incidentally had formerly been the home of Charles Kingsley, author of *The Water Babies*.

At the outset of the 1999 season, thirteen trainers were based in Middleham with the local racehorse population fluctuating between 400 and 450. Johnston's fellow trainers were Ernie Weymes (who was to announce his retirement during the year), James Bethell, Chris Fairhurst, Sally Hall, Micky Hammond, Patrick Haslam, Don Enrico Incisa, Steve Kettlewell, Kate Milligan, George Moore, Ferdy Murphy (whose stable star French Holly was reportedly being aimed at the Cheltenham Gold Cup in March 2000) and Chris Thornton (based at Guy Reed's Spigot Lodge, formerly home to the late Sam Hall, a big-handicap specialist who finished second to the great Noel Murless in the 1960 trainers' table).

All are fortunate to have access to the Low Moor and High Moor gallops, the former boasting a seven-furlong all-weather strip and the latter a mile and a half all-weather track.

CHAPTER TWO

Early Days

A qualified vet, Johnston's training operation had initially been based at Bank End Stables, North Somercotes in Lincolnshire. The establishment then comprised Mark, Deirdre, two members of staff, plus twenty boxes and a half-dozen horses. The shoreline was utilised as gallops, care being taken not to exercise when bombing training was in progress! Initial success came when Hinari Video, a two-year-old colt by Sallust, won at Carlisle in July 1987. Even at that early stage, Johnston's ambition and self-belief were almost limitless. He recalls how he sought to draw attention to himself at the sales by having Deirdre call, asking for him to be paged, ensuring the tannoy boomed "Would Mark Johnston, the trainer, please go to the…," etc. Johnston's ambition and that of his partners was such that when Kingsley House was acquired a massive (and ongoing) programme of investment in new and upgraded facilities was undertaken to transform a rundown thirty-four box yard into one of the most impressive training facilities in the country, with an on-site equine pool, electronic horse walkers and a veterinary room with endoscope and x-ray facilities.

Johnston thought Middleham an ideal base largely because of the quality of the natural training grounds on the Low and High Moors but also for hard-headed commercial reasons. The town is ideally situated from the stand-point of travel to most racecourses throughout the country, allowing owners substantial savings on training expenses in comparison with the large southern bases at Newmarket and Lambourn.

Steady progress was made through 1989-1991, horses such as Hinari Televideo, Craft Express and Lifewatch Vision adding to Mark's growing reputation.

A first Group race success for the yard was achieved in 1992 by Marina Park, a two-year-old filly by Local Suitor, who landed the Group 3 Princess Margaret Stakes at Ascot in July. Johnston believes that this win was particularly important in establishing his credibility at the highest level, as Group success for northern trainers had become something of a rarity. Marina Park went on to finish third to Zafonic in the Prix Morny at Deauville in August and second to Forest Wind in the Mill Reef Stakes in September.

1992 also witnessed the rise to fame of Quick Ransom, a game chestnut, who'd cost just 6,000 gns as a yearling. The balance of his form at two and three years hadn't really hinted at the improvement which was to come. However, in 1992, the gelding's progress was remarkable and his consis-tency a credit to all at Kingsley House. Quick Ransom ran eleven times, beginning by winning handicaps at Haydock and York, then finishing runner-up in the Northern Dancer Handicap at Epsom and the Old Newton Cup at Haydock before the end of July. His 'purple patch' came in August and September when he secured back-to-back victories in the Tote Ebor Handicap at York and Ascot's Krug Trophy Handicap, netting £133,180 in the process. Timeform's *Racehorses of 1992* summed up his year by declaring that "a tougher, more genuine and consistent handicapper would be hard to find". The following season Quick Ransom won a handicap at York in June before justifying favouritism in the William Hill November Handicap at Doncaster, taking his earnings at that stage to £214,787. His career at six was notable for an abortive spring campaign in the USA (he struck into himself and went lame on his first run), an audacious attempt at the Foster's Melbourne Cup in Australia and success in the 'Pitmens' Derby', the Newcastle Brown Ale Northumberland Plate. Tried also in pattern company, he chased home Arcadian Heights in the Doncaster Cup.

Halfway through 1992 Mark took over the training of Branston Abby, a three-year-old filly by Risk Me. She was to become something of a legend in the stable and the yardstick against which all of Johnston's future sprinters were tested. The winner of twenty-four of her ninety-nine runs, including ten listed races, this mare was, at one time, memorably and favourably likened to another "durable and much-loved northern female", Coronation Street's Bet Gilroy, in Timeform's *Racehorses of 1995*. Although highly-strung, Branston Abby was thoroughly genuine, and the aggressive manner in which she was campaigned over the years and the geographical spread of the races she contested (from Carlisle to Sha Tin via Evry, Munich and Rome) typified Johnston's approach to training. Sadly, the mare was to contract acute grass sickness early in her retirement, and she died in May 1997. Her remains are buried at Kingsley House where a gravestone has been erected in her memory.

In 1993, Johnston acquired his first Arab-owned horse named Pearl Kite, a Silver Hawk two-year-old filly owned by Saeed Manana and managed by Sheikh Mohammed's Darley Stud team. She won a York maiden on her debut on 1st September and since then the yard has continued to enjoy the patronage of the Maktoum family and their associates. Researching Pearl Kite's record reminded me of Mark's tale of persistence as to how he courted and achieved such patronage. He wrote to Sheikh Mohammed looking for a job after he qualified but before he became a trainer. When he received no reply he also wrote directly to Anthony Stroud of Darley Stud Management urging him to consider sending horses to Middleham for Mark to train. Heading for Tattersalls Sales at Newmarket on one occasion and armed with copies of those letters Johnston sought out His Highness and promptly presented him with them for his further attention. Although no immediate reply was forthcoming there's little doubt his directness and self-confidence impressed the recipient and led, directly or indirectly, to their current association.

By the end of 1993 it had become clear that Johnston was on the brink of major success. He'd sent out the winners of seventy-seven races to a value of £364,422 and, amongst a group of successful Kingsley House two-year-olds, were two colts whose future exploits would establish their trainer amongst the front rank of his profession and put Middleham firmly back on the racing map: Mister Baileys and Double Trigger.

Mister Baileys, a colt by Robellino, was purchased for just 10,500 gns after failing to reach his reserve price at the Newmarket October Yearling Sales. The winner of three of his five races as a two-year-old, a maiden race at Newcastle in June in which he made a major impression, the Group 3 Champagne Stakes at Goodwood and the Group 2 Royal Lodge Stakes at Ascot, Mister Baileys had his connections dreaming of Classic success over the long winter months. There had been a valid excuse for his first defeat at Newbury, where jockey Dean McKeown had been boxed in on the rails. Additionally, when disappointing in the Gimcrack Stakes at York, he was probably suffering from the after-effects of a ringworm infection. Such was owner Paul Venner's confidence in the horse, he turned down several lucrative offers during the winter. After a cold, wet spring which severely hampered preparations it was decided to let the colt take his chance in the 2000 Guineas without the benefit of a prep race. Johnston recalls that one month prior to the race he had not been able to get a single serious gallop into Mister Baileys, who was being kept active by utilising the seven-furlong all-weather strip on the Low Moor. However, the weather relented at last and early in April Mister Baileys was finally able to work on turf. From that moment on he began to improve markedly, and when his regular work companion Arak won decisively at Thirsk two weeks before the Guineas, optimism within the stable grew, fuelled further by impressive racecourse gallops at the same course and Ripon.

Prior to the Royal Lodge Dean McKeown left Britain to take up a lucrative new job in Hong Kong and the ride on Mister Baileys was offered to Frankie Dettori. The plan had been to utilise Dettori's services in the Newmarket Classic too, but, following the suspension of Pat Eddery, who was due to partner Grand Lodge for William Jarvis, the Italian deserted the Middleham colt and opted for that horse instead. Johnston had recently appointed Jason Weaver as stable jockey, and, despite his youth, it was decided to entrust the most important ride in Johnston's career to date to him. Dettori's preference for Grand Lodge was perhaps understandable, Lord Howard de Walden's colt having topped the Free Handicap and the Two Year Old International Classifications in 1993 and having had the benefit of a previous run that season. However, Frankie's choice was to prove an error of judgement as Mister Baileys blazed the trail from pillar to post, holding off Grand Lodge by a short head with Colonel Collins a further three lengths adrift in third. In winning Middleham's first Classic since 1945 Mister Baileys also set a new track record of 1m 35.08sec. It seemed fitting that he was owned by Paul Venner of Bailey's Horse Feeds. Venner had been Johnston's first owner. Furthermore, his company's products and the feeding regime devised by Mark had proved one of the cornerstones of the yard's success. The victory also catapulted Weaver into the limelight and provided him with a launch pad for further success at the top level throughout the nineties.

Despite Mister Baileys appearing not to stay when beaten four and a half lengths into third behind Erhaab in the Homeowners' Dante Stakes over ten and a half furlongs at York, Johnston pleaded with Paul Venner that the horse be allowed to take his chance in the Derby all the same. Mark recalls sending him a three-page letter arguing the case for the colt to run in the blue riband of the turf. When at last the owner consented, preparations for the big race included galloping Mister Baileys the 'wrong way' round Middleham Moor to simulate the left-handed downhill approach to Epsom's Tattenham Corner. In the event, despite the doubt about the horse's stamina, Jason Weaver rode an attacking race, kicking Mister Baileys into a six-length lead rounding Tattenham Corner, only for the partnership to be collared just below the distance. Johnston still recalls, wryly, that he has never seen a horse so utterly exhausted after a race as Mister Baileys was after the Derby. Yet in finishing fourth to Erhaab, the colt lost little caste in defeat, and the sight of him shooting several lengths clear early in the straight remains one of the abiding memories of the 1994 racing season.

Accepting that the Derby trip was beyond Mister Baileys' compass, Johnston decided that the colt should revert to the Guineas' distance of a mile and targeted the Group 1 Sussex Stakes at Goodwood for his charge. Regrettably, the colt was unable to overcome the effects of an injury to his off-fore sustained in the Derby and finished in mid division. Thus it was decided to retire him to stud. Although due to stand at the National Stud in 1995, Mister Baileys dramatically contracted a life-threatening grass sickness disease before commencing stallion duties. Fortunately, he survived, was sold to stand at Vinery Stud in America and his progeny are now beginning to appear on our racecourses. It was one of Mark's goals for 1999 that he should train the first of them to win a race.

Double Trigger had been purchased for just 7,200 guineas at the Irish National Yearling Sales. A chestnut colt by Ela-Mana-Mou, Double Trigger was undefeated as a two-year-old, capturing a Redcar maiden over nine furlongs and Newmarket's Sporting Life Zetland Stakes over ten furlongs, the manner of victory in both suggesting that a future star in the stayers' division had arrived. Despite such promise, Double Trigger's career as a three-year-old proved something of an anticlimax as he was beset by injuries which kept him off the course until August. A kick from his stable-companion Quick Ransom was only one of the problems with which his trainer had to deal. He eventually lined up for the Great Voltigeur Stakes at York and, though only fifth, was beaten just two lengths by the winner,

Sacrament. However, the good to firm ground on the Knavesmire added to his problems, giving him sore shins. In the circumstances, third place in the Teleconnection St Leger at Doncaster, where he finished four and a quarter lengths behind Moonax, was something of a triumph. Success in the St Leger Italiano at Turin in November followed, Double Trigger seeing off the challenge of the French-trained Michel Georges by three and a half lengths. The curtain came down on his season in Hong Kong's International Vase over a mile and a half, in which he finished in mid division behind Red Bishop.

If 1994 had been a year of frustration for Double Trigger's connections, what satisfaction they must have derived from his four-year-old campaign in 1995, when he achieved the stayers' Triple Crown, winning the Ascot Gold Cup, Goodwood Cup and Doncaster Cup. After a narrow victory in the Insulpak Sagaro Stakes at Ascot, Double Trigger finished only fourth in the Yorkshire Cup behind Moonax, clearly unsuited by reverting to a mile and three quarters (although it must be said that Johnston always held Moonax in very high regard). Back over two miles at Sandown, Double Trigger ran away with the Bonusprint Henry II Stakes, as a result of which he lined up at Ascot at a starting price of 9/4, behind only Moonax (13/8) in the betting. Double Trigger turned in a devastating front-running performance, quickening over four furlongs out to defeat his St Leger and Yorkshire Cup conqueror by five lengths.

In the next leg of his Triple Crown attempt 'Trigger' met his stable-mate and younger full brother Double Eclipse, who had emulated his two-year-old success in Newmarket's Zetland Stakes. Double Eclipse had had an indifferent season prior to Goodwood, albeit having been campaigned at the highest level. He had run in the Prix Hocquart at Longchamp and the Budweiser Irish Derby without making much impression, but a neck second to Stelvio in the Queen's Vase at Royal Ascot over two miles clearly signalled his potential for top-class achievement in the staying division. At Goodwood Double Eclipse ran the race of his life, and after an epic battle with his brother throughout the final quarter of a mile, went down by only a neck. Double Trigger was conceding 6 lb more than weight-for-age and the sight of the pair fighting out the finish of a Cup race and, what's more, giving their all in a searing drive to the line, is still vivid in Mark's memory.

When Double Trigger took the East Coast Doncaster Cup in September he became only the fourth horse this century to land the stayers' Triple Crown, joining Alycidon, Le Moss (twice) and Longboat. After a relatively disappointing run in Longchamp's Prix du Cadran Double Trigger was found to have a lung infection and probably still wasn't spot on when disappointing in the Melbourne Cup in Australia. There, under top weight of 9 st 7 lb and starting at 7/2 favourite, he failed to fire and was eased considerably towards the finish, concern over irregularities in a pre-race blood sample having additionally soured the experience.

Although Double Trigger's 1996 campaign began with victories in the Insulpak Sagaro Stakes at Ascot and the Bonusprint Henry II Stakes at Sandown, his attempt to emulate Le Moss and repeat that Triple Crown success failed. In the Ascot Gold Cup, Double Trigger was outpaced by Godolphin's Classic Cliche and went under by one and a half lengths. Much criticism was levelled at Jason Weaver for failing to make more use of the horse, allowing Classic Cliche's superior speed to become the decisive factor in the finish. Johnston himself did not agree with this analysis. In the aftermath it came to light that Trigger had lost his off-fore shoe during the race, damaging the hoof, as a result of which he was sidelined until September. Given that this injury was to take months to resolve itself, the Ascot defeat was quickly forgiven, especially as he bounced back to form in the East Coast Doncaster Cup in September, beating Celeric by two lengths in record time under an enterprising ride from Frankie Dettori. A further bid was made for the Prix du Cadran but again Double Trigger failed to sparkle in the Bois du Boulogne.

Double Trigger's 1997 season saw him triumph from adversity when landing another memorable win in the Goodwood Cup. The horse had struggled to find his form in the face of continuing injury problems, including foot abscesses and the discovery of an irregular heartbeat. At Goodwood, however, he showed his best form under a forceful ride from Michael Roberts, drawing clear of his old rival Classic Cliche to win cosily by a length and a half. Buoyed by this success, Johnston dispatched 'Trigger' to Paris but alas his Prix du Cadran jinx continued. On this occasion Michael Roberts' plane arrived late and leading French jockey Thierry Jarnet was asked to step in at short notice. The partnership was not an instant success, and whilst the trainer was clear that Jarnet understood his instructions he later asked rhetorically "How do you explain Trigger to a French jockey?"

Thus, now seven, Double Trigger entered 1998 with something to prove, and when failing to make the frame in his now traditional pipe-openers at Newmarket (where the Sagaro Stakes was relocated) and Sandown the knockers were out in force. At Sandown in particular his challenge had been tame and he returned from the race with swollen fore legs. It was hardly surprising that he was allowed to start at 25/1 for the Ascot Gold Cup, taking his place in a field which was not only the largest of the century up until that point (16) but also of rare quality, no fewer than eleven of the participants boasting pattern victories. Thus, in addition to Trigger and previous winner Celeric, the field contained the last two winners of the Queen's Vase (Windsor Castle and Gordi), the latest winners of the Chester Cup (Silence in Court), Park Hill Stakes (Book at Bedtime), September Stakes (Maylane), Doncaster Cup (Canon Can), Ormonde Stakes (Stretarez), Prix de Lutece (Three Cheers) and Henry II Stakes (Persian Punch, who started favourite) and the 1996 Ebor winner, Clerkenwell. Double Trigger's new partner, Darryll Holland, kicked on approaching the home turn, burning off most of his illustrious rivals and although Kayf Tara took over the lead at the distance the old horse refused to give best and renewed his effort in a memorable race to the line. At the post, he was beaten only a neck by Godolphin's four-year-old.

After that sterling effort, Double Trigger went straight for the Goodwood Cup. Despite seemingly back-pedalling early in the straight, he was galvanised into producing a doughty and stirring late run by Holland, whose efforts were subsequently recognised by his peers at the 'Lesters', and, at the winning post, had three quarters of a length to spare over Canon Can, with Kayf Tara back in fifth. Double Trigger's distinguished career came to a fitting end on September 10th 1998, when he ran out the winner of the GNER Doncaster Cup by a length and two and a half lengths from Busy Flight and Canon Can, in the process becoming the first horse since Beeswing in 1841 (the mare also won the race the following year) to win the prize three times. Emotional scenes followed as his lad Geordie Charlton brought the hero of the hour back to the winner's enclosure. 'Trigger' had established a special place in the hearts of the Flat racing public. As the winner of the Cartier and Racegoers Club awards, it has always annoyed Johnston that the official handicapper's ratings did not do justice to his stable star. Ask him to argue the case for 'Trigger' as the horse of the decade and he will not be short of debating points!

Sadly, it transpired that Double Trigger had struck into himself, injuring a tendon, which effectively ruled out one last attempt at the Cadran. Nonetheless, he completed his career as the winner of fourteen races worth a total of £431,211. These successes included seven in "Cup" races, one more than Le Moss who had completed the stayers' Triple Crown in both 1979 and 1980. Double Trigger's final success in the Doncaster Cup took his total of pattern race victories to twelve, a total bettered amongst horses trained in Britain and Ireland since the introduction of the pattern system in 1971 only by Brigadier Gerard and Ardross. Johnston summed up his impact: "I may win bigger races than the Goodwood Cup and Doncaster Cup, but it's hard to imagine that I will ever train a bigger star than Double Trigger!"

Timeform conferred a fitting tribute upon Double Trigger in *Racehorses of 1998,* in which, in summary of his long and illustrious career they declared: "He was a relentless stayer and a great battler and racing as a whole will be the poorer for his retirement." Double Trigger was a special racehorse, and the manner in which he was taken to the public's heart was almost unique for a Flat performer in recent times.

Following Mister Baileys and Double Trigger came Bijou d'Inde, a chestnut colt by Cadeaux Genereux. Bought for 20,000 gns as a yearling, the colt was to prove a real bargain for his astute owner, Glasgow solicitor and business-man Stuart Morrison, whose colours had been carried by Quick Ransom. After two narrow defeats in maiden company in 1995, Bijou d'Inde pro-gressed to win the Acomb Stakes at the York Ebor meeting before lifting the Group 3 Futurity Stakes at the Curragh. The plan for the colt to emulate Mister Baileys by winning the Royal Lodge Stakes at Ascot was frustrated by a bout of lameness during his preparation. Though he recovered well enough to take his place, he was clearly not firing on all cylinders, finishing a disappointing fifth behind Mons.

Ante-post betting activity for the 1996 2000 Guineas centred around Alhaarth, champion two-year-old of 1995, when the winner of all his five races, including the Dewhurst Stakes, and Beauchamp King, the Craven Stakes winner. Prior to the classic Bijou d'Inde's jockey Jason Weaver reported to Morrison that the 'buzz' amongst some of his fellow riders was that Alhaarth had failed to train on. The Middleham challenger was despatched to Newmarket with Johnston expecting a big run. He didn't disappoint and, in a frenetic, driving finish, failed by a short head and a head against Mark of Esteem and Even Top. The riding of all three jockeys involved in the battle to the line, Dettori, Robinson and Weaver, earned them a suspension for misuse of the whip. Frankie Dettori, on the winner, was banned for no less than eight days! Alhaarth and Beauchamp King finished fourth and fifth, six lengths behind Bijou d'Inde.

A lost shoe and much softer going contributed to an unsuccessful bid to land the Irish 2000 Guineas, in the circumstances fourth place behind Spinning World being a useful effort. And so to Royal Ascot! The 1996 St

James's Palace Stakes brought together the winners of the English, Irish and French 2000 Guineas in Mark of Esteem, Spinning World and Ashkalani, together with Beauchamp King and Cayman Kai, a close fourth in France. In another memorable drive to the line, Bijou d'Inde's determination proved decisive as he outbattled Ashkalani close home, in the process gaining deserved compensation for that narrow Newmarket reverse.

An audacious plan to land another Group 1 prize just eighteen days later in the Coral-Eclipse Stakes at Sandown over ten furlongs was hatched. Bidding to become the first three-year-old to capture the St James's Palace Stakes and Eclipse for sixty years, he failed by only a neck to hold Godolphin's five-year-old Halling. Although his subsequent efforts were a little disappointing (third in the International at York and sixth in the Queen Elizabeth II Stakes at Ascot), it was decided to winter the horse in Dubai with a view to a tilt at the 1997 Dubai World Cup. Regrettably, in the World Cup itself Bijou d'Inde was brought down, in the process damaging a tendon, an injury which was to reduce the colt's effectiveness. Nonetheless, at the end of that season he was syndicated for £1m and currently stands at Woodlands Stud, Newmarket. His first runners will be on the track in 2001.

Gothenberg, a bay colt by Polish Patriot, who cost just 5,700 gns as a yearling and raced for Brian Yeardley Continental Limited, was another renowned inmate of Kingsley House, winning seven of his thirty-six races from five to eight furlongs between 1995 and 1998, including a listed race at Epsom at two, the Lexus Tetrarch Stakes and Sea World International Stakes at the Curragh at three, then Group 2 races at Milan and Hoppegarten the following year. He had career earnings of £288,180, and is now at Easthorpe Hall Stud in Malton.

Last but not least, no summary of Johnston's best horses to date could leave out Princely Heir and Lend A Hand, colts who provided Group 1 successes for the stable as two-year-olds in 1997. Lend A Hand won the Gran Criterium at Milan by seven and a half lengths before joining the Godolphin empire and Princely Heir lifted the Heinz 57 Phoenix Stakes at Leopardstown. The latter remained in training at Kingsley House at the start of 1999.

No doubt many of you have memories of other Kingsley House stalwarts whose feats haven't been recounted here—Millstream, Jural and Double Blue to name but three. However, these reflections should be regarded as providing a flavour of the success engendered by Johnston to date.

Asked to name his 'favourite' five horses at the outset of the 1999 season, Johnston quickly reeled off Branston Abby, Gothenberg and Quick Ransom as those who had given him the most fun. Typical of the man, he went on to explain that this was not just because of the exploits of these horses themselves, all of whom improved by leaps and bounds, but because of the sporting attitude and demeanour of their respective owners, David Abell, Brian Yeardley and Stuart Morrison. How typical of Johnston's attitude towards training that he should select three out of his favourite five horses on the basis of the fun engendered for their owners!

He nominates Mister Baileys as the fourth member simply because "he's the best horse I've ever trained". Needless to say, the last pick is Double Trigger. Asked to sum up why, Johnston encapsulates a thousand headaches, worries, emotions, concerns, sleepless nights and tears of joy in four words: "because he was special."

But would 1999 yield another 'special' horse for Middleham and Johnston?

CHAPTER THREE

The Team

Attention to detail. For Mark Johnston this is the key to his remarkable success over the last ten years and a factor which distinguishes his training operation from most of its potential competitors. Standards of horse husbandry set by Johnston are high. Very high. Quizzed about his secondary and tertiary education, Johnston is inclined to be self-effacing. University entrance qualifications were not easily achieved, the academic fruits of his school career requiring to be augmented by further highers undertaken at Glasgow's Cardonald College of Further Education. Take him at his word and his graduating from the University of Glasgow Vet School came as a surprise both to him and to certain of his contemporaries. Excuses to avoid knuckling down to work were sought at every turn, he says. He even tells a compelling story of how a journey with a like-minded colleague across Glasgow by Corporation Bus to a dreaded 'meat examination' class at Glasgow's slaughterhouse off Duke Street in Dennistoun turned into a hitch hiking trip to Paris! Those of us who reside in the "dear green place" can only marvel at the manifestation of such imagination on the top deck of a bus as it lurched past the Glasgow Necropolis, Tennent Caledonian's pungent Wellgate Brewery, the Great

Eastern Hotel (a model lodging house) and Duke Street Hospital! One also wonders at which bus stop the adventurers chose to alight as offering the best prospects of a lift to Paris in Glasgow's East End! Yet, spend an hour in Johnston's company on Middleham's gallops and you will be left in no doubt as to his feeling for horses and his ability to spot from a distance even the most minor veterinary problem. This is a man for whom the wellbeing of the horses in his care is paramount, and it is testament to his success in this field that the business should have grown so rapidly in recent years. Perhaps the Paris trip and similar jaunts should be viewed in a more positive light as having sown the seeds in Johnston's psyche of the idea that his charges should be campaigned where the rewards are greatest, regardless of distance, another of the distinctive features of Johnston's *modus operandi*!

How does this attention to detail manifest itself, you may ask? Well, go to Middleham and see for yourself. Stay at the Waterford House Hotel in Kirkgate (that's one you owe me, Brian and Everyll!). Watch first lot pull out just after 6 am. Each rider will be well turned out in Mark Johnston Racing Limited branded clothing. Tack and rugs will be pristine and the string will make its way past the hotel and on toward the Low Moor in a well-disciplined manner. Either Mark Johnston or his assistant/vet Susanna Ballinger will see each horse before it canters; any horse which has been coughing or which is showing signs of lameness, however slight, will be sent home, always presuming that it has left the yard before being spotted by one of the senior members of staff. Indeed, administration manager Debbie Albion is often to be seen dashing from her desk in the office out into the yard if she has any concern regarding the soundness of a horse as it passes the office door.

On the Moor, horses work as directed; woe betide anyone who fails to have theirs upsides when directed by Johnston to do so. If there is any doubt about conditions Johnston walks the tracks, all-weather or grass, and decisions as to where the morning's work will take place are made on the basis of that. Indeed, I can claim to have assisted Mark in a two-man operation to remove grazing sheep from part of the High Moor five furlong turf gallop to allow Fez and her companions to work prior to her run in the Flying Childers! Mark also often cycles over the gallops these days, claiming that it is a great way to feel the bumps!

At the races, a Johnston runner will stand out more often than not. The trademark signs? Beautifully turned out, big, round, shiny, fit horses which are benefiting from the yard's tried and tested regime of extra feed for extra work, kitted out in smart, clean tack (including white breastgirths) and led up by well-groomed, conscientious staff. Awards for the best turned out horse are regularly won. Above all, the attention to detail is reflected in Johnston's own thoughtfulness regarding his charges. Susanna Ballinger refers to her boss as a perfectionist. Self criticism is part of his makeup and drives him on remorselessly. Never a day passes during the flat racing season without him studying the trainers' table in the *Racing Post*, analysing his statistics, reflecting upon perceived failures, making strategies to improve results and worrying about the future. During the 1999 Ebor meeting (mid-August) he commented to me that he is not complacent and does not take past successes as a guarantee of future security. He is acutely aware that unless his organisation continues to strive for success at all levels his recent elevation to the higher echelons of the trainers' table is unlikely to be maintained. He expressed relief that, having achieved 75 winners up until that point, any potential 'collapse' wouldn't happen next year. This may be the attitude of a self-critical perfectionist, but it is also that of a realistic, feet-on-the-ground Scot and, make no mistake, Johnston is a Scot who regards himself as forced to live in exile by the demands of his profession. Not only does Johnston take the time and trouble to reflect upon statistics, he constantly searches for solutions which would have the effect of improving them. With approximately one-hundred-and-fifty horses in training at any one time and a staff complement of over seventy-five people the running of Mark Johnston Racing Limited demands an organisational structure that gets the best out of the horses by first getting the best out of its staff. In his introduction to the stable's 1998 Staff Handbook, Johnston comments that "in order to reach out for the very top of this industry we have to have a team of people second to none … we will work together to develop our staff into the best team in the land".

Johnston's determination to develop the skills and experience of his staff further is evident, and Rory McDonald, Director of the British Racing School, is employed on a consultancy basis to assist with the training and development programme. As part of his initial input Johnston was persuaded that the adoption of a company logo and motto might provide a catalyst around which all sorts of developments might take place—greater public awareness of the business, a greater feeling of 'belonging' among the staff, etc. When asked to think of a motto Johnston's mind returned to Hamilton Park Racecourse, where he has become accustomed over the years to being asked by the astute local punters in hushed conspiratorial tones "is it trying, son?" The reflex (and honest) reply—"we're always trying"—thrust itself forward as the obvious slogan for the job!

It is an expression which typifies Johnston's attitude to training, racing and administration. In handling staff matters, whilst he is a strict disciplinarian, he will always acknowledge effort on the part of his employees, particularly that of a team member who is clearly working to improve his or her contribution to the business.

In the early part of his career, Mark was struck by the number of tales he heard about owners arriving at racecourses, often with guests in tow, only to be told by their trainers that their horses were "not off today". Given that most horses don't run more than six times a season, Johnston felt that this practice effectively short-changed owners. He saw a niche and decided to promote his business on the basis that his horses would always be trying. Furthermore, his veterinary training, together with a close observation of racehorses over the years, has led him to believe that horses are either leaders or followers. Thus their training should always seek to capitalise on these instincts. He tries to instil in his charges a heightened awareness of the distinctive atmosphere of the racecourse and hopes that when setting foot on the track they will always experience an adrenalin buzz. Thus if horses were to be given "a quiet run" Mark would be concerned that losing habits might be acquired.

To focus this ethos of effort further, and to provide a yardstick against which progress can be measured, Johnston has always set himself goals, even from his earliest days training in Lincolnshire. These targets relate to achievement on the track, achievement in the fields of horse husbandry and staff development and also to the financial control of the business. Budgetary targets are set in November/December and are never changed. The principal goals for achievement on the track are set in a manner which will challenge the staff and Johnston himself to push onwards for further success and not simply to rest on their laurels.

At the start of 1999 the triple targets set by Johnston were to train at least a century of winners, to win £1 million in prize money in Britain alone and to train at least one Group 1 winner. Most of the remainder of this book charts the progress towards those goals and observes how Johnston and his team responded to the challenges posed by them. In his Staff Handbook Johnston likens himself to a centre forward in football, "scoring" the goals but requiring support from his team to do so. On the one hand this analogy seems appropriate, but on the other in many ways his role might be more aptly likened to that of a premiership manager. Not only is he responsible for the assembly of the team, their physical and mental preparation, tactics, dealing with the media, etc., but he also requires to consider every aspect of his craft and the 'players' in his care with a view to securing every possible advantage for his team. This could relate to race planning, discussing handicap marks with a BHB handicapper or using the press to his advantage, for example. We will see an example of the latter when we come to reflect on Fruits of Love's preparation for the King George.

The key members of Johnston's team bring a potent mixture of youthful enthusiasm and mature experience to Middleham's premier outfit. In many ways, Mark's wife Deirdre has a number of very difficult and disparate functions to perform within the business. Not only is she a director of Mark Johnston Racing Limited, she also rides out every morning and indeed is the regular pilot of Fruits of Love. Her skills in liaison with owners and the media are a most valuable asset to the business and her own insistence on the highest of standards from the staff reinforces and complements her husband's focus on attention to detail. She often represents the stable on the racecourse and perhaps her biggest contribution to the success of the business lies in her providing a sounding board for Mark as they bounce ideas about running plans, etc., around. When riding out Deirdre is often able to observe the string at close hand, not only during work but also on the way to and from the gallops. As the walk from Kingsley House to Middleham's High Moor can take a half hour or so, this presents an additional opportunity for Deirdre to judge the wellbeing (or otherwise) of the string and the performance of the staff. She will also often raise points arising from such observations at the Tuesday morning management meetings and she is very much 'hands on' in her approach to her directorial role. Just for good measure, she combines all of these tasks with being a housewife and mother to Charlie and Angus too!

Mark and Deirdre's fellow directors in Mark Johnston Racing Limited are their long-term friends and supporters, Brian and Val Palmer, who have a non-executive role. Although not directly involved in racing operations Brian's influence in the business will be clear to those who remember the early days of Johnston's regime when a number of horses ran under the "Hinari" prefix, as Brian was in the domestic electrical business trading under the highly successful "Hinari Consumer Electrics Limited" banner.

Susanna Ballinger is employed as the stable's resident veterinary surgeon/assistant trainer. An ex-pupil of Epsom College and a graduate of Bristol University Veterinary School, Susanna was working for the bloodstock section of the *Racing Post* when she decided, not altogether seriously, to respond to an advertisement which had been placed by Mark Johnston Racing Limited. Granted an interview, she impressed Johnston sufficiently to be offered the job and has made herself an integral part of the continuing success story. She is responsible for the vet diary and the day-to-day care of the horses. On occasions, she saddles the stable's runners on course and during Johnston's absence will also prepare the work lists, which is no easy task in a stable of this size. Around a hundred and fifty horses require to gallop, canter, swim, exercise on the horse walkers or simply be mucked out in their boxes each day. Suitable riders have to be matched to horses. For example, an inexperienced member of staff is not asked to ride a horse which has shown an unwillingness to jump off at the beginning of a piece of work. If, as is usual, Mark is preparing the list and is undecided as to the level of work to be set for a particular horse he will often inspect it in its box before finalising his decision. In Middleham the choice of gallops available is another variable to be taken into account. Three factors in particular contrive to make Susanna's job a difficult one. Firstly, as a result of the stable's policy to feed horses well and demand more work from them, there is always the danger of an injury rate amongst its horses that is higher than average. Thus a close watch is required to be kept by Susanna, and the vet diary records not only her own comments but those of other senior staff too. Much use is made of endoscopy, where appropriate, and the horses' weights are regularly checked and recorded.

A second complicating factor is of course that Mark is a qualified vet and thus there are frequent opportunities for conflict to arise between Susanna and Mark as regards diagnosis and treatment. Without personalising these opportunities for conflict, it could perhaps be suggested that 'new methods, theory and youth' may compete with 'traditional methods and experience'. To the credit of both Johnston and Ballinger, however, these exchanges of opinion are largely taken in good part. In practice, Susanna will take most routine decisions on her own initiative, subject to the overall scrutiny of Johnston, and will defend vigorously the decisions she has made to the trainer. At the same time, Johnston takes a very proactive approach to the vet diary. Throughout the year, whenever I saw him in possession of a printout, it was always heavily annotated and marked with his own points of concern.

Lastly, the demarcation of Susanna's functions as assistant trainer is to a certain extent affected by Deirdre's roving commission within the management structure. In particular, her involvement in racing operations can be restricted. However, the flexibility and team spirit which permeates the management team seems to ensure that no undue tension arises despite the apparent overlap in their respective roles.

The fact that the business retains a resident vet is further testament to the stated aim of attention to detail, and I spoke to two owners in the course of the season who indicated to me that the availability of a resident vet at the stable had played a major part in their deciding to place horses with Johnston.

The Head Lad is Brendan Holland, who hails from Blarney, County Cork. Brendan holds a degree in agriculture and is a solid, unflappable and laid-back individual. He is in overall control of both yards and has particular responsibility for feeding, weighing and farrier matters. Married, with a first child due at the end of the year, Brendan is known as 'Blarney' to the staff. Needless to say he is not slow to express his views on matters affecting the business, and does so most eloquently. Brendan also represents the yard at the racecourse from time to time.

Working under Brendan are the two Second Head Lads, Jock Bennett and Debbie Kettlewell. Jock Bennett has been in racing for twenty-five years. A resident of Richmond, he worked as Head Lad to local trainer Bill Watts, of Teleprompter fame, before joining Johnston's operation when Watts decided to call it a day. Solid and dependable, Jock has had a broad experience in racing and sets a good example to the younger members of staff. As Second Head Lad, he is responsible for the Kingsley House horses and for the Blue staff team. Obviously, Jock liaises with Brendan Holland and with the administration manager on a daily basis, but he is also asked to attend the Tuesday meetings, at which agenda items include as a matter of course weekly reports from him on the horses under his care and any staff issues arising relating to the Blue team.

The Warwick House yard is home to the stable's two-year-old army and the Second Head Lad in charge of that brigade is Debbie Kettlewell. When Mark and Deirdre first set up in Lincolnshire, Debbie, who has ridden successfully as an amateur on the flat and over hurdles, was part of their original team. She left to marry trainer Steve Kettlewell, but when that relationship ended in divorce was happy to return to the Johnstons and is now in control of the Warwick House yard and the Green staff team. Debbie's enthusiasm for the horses in her care is obvious. Like Jock, she attends the Tuesday meeting and is always forthright in her views regarding her horses and their wellbeing.

The stable is particularly well served in the role of Travelling Head Lass by Robynne Watton. Robynne is very quiet by nature and is often ribbed by fellow staff for her reserved, almost unsmiling demeanour. However, she is the living embodiment of the stable's ethos of attention to detail, taking a real pride in her work. She is the winner of countless awards as the person responsible for the 'best turned out' horse in a race, and such is the trust that Johnston has in her judgement that when Bijou d'Inde ran in the Dubai World Cup of 1997, he was happy to leave her in control and to allow her to accompany the horse to Dubai to oversee his preparation in the weeks prior to the race. Robynne is responsible for all travel matters and attends to every aspect of her work with great diligence. She also rides out whenever possible. High opinions of Robynne's merit extend outside the stable itself. Indeed she was voted the Horserace Writers & Photographers Association Stable Hand of the Year at the end of 1999.

Bobby Elliott is in charge of jockey matters and is also the yard's senior work rider. A man of few words, Elliott's role is vital in that he is able to provide Johnston with a rider's insight into the string and the wellbeing of the horses.

Champion apprentice in 1959 and 1960, he is a skilled horseman respected throughout the industry. Bobby had notable success at Royal Ascot, partnering winners of the Royal Hunt Cup, the Wokingham Stakes and the Ascot Stakes and, in the early 'sixties, he also rode successfully for the Queen. Bobby also boasts the distinction of having ridden the great Brigadier Gerard at exercise for Dick Hern—unfortunately he was unceremoniously dumped on the gallops by the great one! Bobby had a wide-ranging career, enjoying spells with Lewes trainer Tom Masson, who had a reputation for handling difficult horses, as well as stints in Hong Kong and the United States. Upon his return to Great Britain his career stuttered somewhat until forming a liaison with the emerging Johnston stable. In six seasons Bobby rode fifty-eight winners for Mark before quitting the saddle in 1993. Owners and their representatives, notably Joe Mercer and Bruce Raymond who manage horses for Maktoum al Maktoum, know Bobby and respect his opinion. Indeed, it was Bobby who partnered Johnston's first winner as a trainer, Hinari Video, at Carlisle back in the summer of 1987 and who alerted Mark to the potential availability of Kingsley House.

Other regular work riders include Joe Fanning and stable apprentice Robbie Fitzpatrick. In the early part of 1999, leading South African jockey Pierre Strydom also rode out, whilst Tyrone Williams and Paul Fessey were called upon when needed. Johnston no longer retains a stable jockey but at the start of the season it was fair to assume that the one likely to be offered most rides would be Darryll Holland. Holland, however, is a resident of Newmarket and an infrequent visitor to Middleham. Fortunately, this does not unduly concern Johnston as he does not regard Holland's greatest asset to be riding work!

A racing organisation of this size demands a sound administrative structure and Mark Johnston Racing Limited is fortunate to have an exceptional individual as Administration Manager in Debbie Albion. Debbie has broad experience within racing. A former Head Lass to Con Horgan, she had several rides as an amateur, and now heads a small administrative team based in a modern purpose-built office at Kingsley House, enjoying the respect of the whole yard.

Debbie is the first point of contact for owners and deals with all aspects of entries, declarations, jockeys etc. She has the unenviable task of pinning the trainer down about decisions on declarations and early-closing races which simply can't wait and is therefore often caught up in a flurry of calls to all involved, including Johnston himself on the gallops. She has a strong personality, a thorough knowledge of racing and horses and, importantly, is not afraid to disagree with Johnston and to make her own views known. She shares Johnston's trait of wishing to have the last word in an argument and thus their verbal exchanges are never dull! She is often to be seen in the yard outside her own working hours and Johnston feels that she "lives for her job" and that she "has a real feel for horses". These traits and the strength of her personality have marked her out to Johnston as someone who ought to be at the heart of a revised organisational structure.... but more of that later!

Although these people form the backbone of Johnston's team, it is important to remember that in racing a team is only as good as its weakest member. Johnston prides himself on the overall quality of his stable staff and currently bucks the trend within racing towards a shortage of employees. Some years ago he devised a system of points scoring, whereby staff earn bonuses through regular timekeeping, volunteering for Sunday racing duty and personal achievement, such as winning a 'best turned out' award. Equally, points are lost through lateness, unauthorised absence, loss or damage to equipment or failing to observe the dress code. Each point is worth £1 and can be exchanged for branded clothing at Race Riders, the local tack shop, which forms part of Warwick House. Johnston holds the view that the introduction of this system, coupled with an insistence that staff clock in, represented a leap forward in staff management. So far as I am aware this type of system is unique to his yard.

Staff are trained not only to deal with the horses to the best of their ability but also to recognise the essential role of owners to the business. Detailed instructions are therefore given in the staff handbook as to how to treat visitors to the yard and how to reinforce the message to the stable's customers that their pivotal role in the business is appreciated in more than one sense of the word.

Before leaving the subject of 'the team', two points have to be stressed. Firstly, Johnston freely admits that he finds the whole area of staff management and performance the most challenging aspect of his job. He has wrestled in his mind many times with the overriding question: should I run the business as a benign (!) dictatorship or should I build in democratic checks and balances? The self-critical, perfectionist aspect of his personality causes him to measure constantly the performance of his staff against his own standards. When he feels that they have not been met, he is frustrated at what he sees as the failure of those concerned to take ownership of their role and to invest the same time, effort and thought. Additionally, he is even more frustrated by what he perceives as a failure on his part to have motivated them better. Those sentiments led to a dramatic change of course before the season ended.

Secondly, although MJRL is run as a team operation, Johnston's natural authority and presence tend to dominate. I am certain that this does not arise from any conscious effort or determination on his part to rule the roost absolutely. He reflects deeply on the responsibilities of command and in my view his style of leadership has arisen as a natural consequence of his sheer hard work and the example of commitment which he gives to his staff. For example, he is often first in and last out and works extremely long hours. I became accustomed to receiving e-mail replies sent by him in the early hours of the morning-all the more impressive when one considers that first lot pulls out at 6 am!

CHAPTER FOUR

January 1999

A sked to reflect on the 1998 season Mark concluded that the performance of his two-year-olds had fallen below expectations and that the older horses, especially Double Trigger, had led the show. On the one hand, therefore, there had to be a concern at the outset of 1999 about the quality of the three-year-olds and whether this might prevent his first goal of 100 winners being reached. Certainly, with the possible exception of Atlantic Destiny and Royal Rebel, there were no obvious potential stars amongst them. Hardly surprising, then, that Johnston felt the target "a tall order, a serious challenge". On the other hand, sober reflection on the performance of the horses had encouraged him to think that the three-year-olds might not be such a bad bunch after all; that they might simply have been slow to mature, and that handicap marks might be seen to be generous once they began to mature. In any event, it would be interesting to see how that group in particular fared once the season began in earnest.

The last racing season of the Millennium began with a festive bang for Mark Johnston Racing Limited at Lingfield on New Year's Day. Both of the stable's runners, Thekryaati and John Bowdler Music, won, at 2/1 and 11/1 respectively. Thekryaati, an Indian Ridge colt who had joined the stable from Ben Hanbury's Newmarket yard, was unraced at two and had run only once as a three-year-old, finishing in midfield in a Newmarket mile maiden in early May. So, when he lifted a ten-furlong maiden a shade cosily under Gary Carter this seemed a very promising start to his Kingsley House career. John Bowdler Music, a more experienced handicapper, was a half-length winner of the appropriately-named Happy New Year Handicap over six furlongs under a strong ride from Joe Fanning, who was completing a double in the process.

The promise shown by Love Diamonds at Wolverhampton on January 6th, when he failed narrowly to hold on in a handicap over a mile and half a furlong, was soon realised. At Lingfield on January 12th under Dean McKeown, he gained a runaway victory over a slightly shorter distance. These early successes were consolidated on January 23rd, the stable enjoying three winners and one second from as many runners, one at Lingfield and two at Wolverhampton.

Three days later, the Hamas gelding, Hormuz, added to the tally at Lingfield, driven clear by Joe Fanning to land a ten-furlong maiden in good style, and the month ended largely as it had begun when Love Blues, a particularly good-looking three-year-old colt, followed up a Wolverhampton success of the previous week by defeating older rivals in grand style in a Classified Stakes at the same course on the 30th, justifying odds-on favouritism by no less than nine lengths under a brisk ride from Jimmy Quinn.

At January's end, the stable's tally stood at 8 wins from 29 runners, a strike rate of 27.6%. If that could be maintained throughout the year Mark's prize-money and winners targets would be achieved easily. Reflecting the relatively poor reward generally on offer on the all-weather circuit, however, the win prize money tally stood at £23,106. Nonetheless, it had been a very good start, by any measure!

CHAPTER FIVE

February 1999

February started well enough when Thekryaati continued his rich vein of form by winning a handicap at Wolverhampton on the 3rd over an extended nine furlongs in decisive style. His record for Johnston's stable now consisted of three wins from four starts, with a valid excuse for his sole defeat at Southwell on his second appearance, when he was crowded.

The yard thought that a second winner for the month was in the bag when Hormuz, attempting to supplement his previous course win, was promoted to first after finishing a short head behind Neil Graham's filly Azihaam in the ten-furlong Margery Allingham Handicap at Lingfield on February 6th. However, the connections of the demoted horse appealed against the decision of the local stewards that Azihaam had hung into Hormuz causing interference, and were represented at the appeal by the trainer's wife, solicitor and Channel 4 racing presenter Lesley Graham. Lesley was clearly able to weave almost as good a story as the famous author whose name had been borrowed by the Lingfield executive for the title of the race and their appeal was upheld! This was, nonetheless, a satisfactory performance from Hormuz.

The second winner of the month arrived on the 12th at Southwell, where the Housebuster colt Kentucky Bullet, unraced at two, landed the spoils at the third time of asking in a seven-furlong maiden, Joe Fanning having pushed him clear just before the distance. Thekryaati's attempt to continue his good run ended in narrow defeat, the colt going down by the minimum distance in a handicap at Lingfield on the 16th.

Thereafter, despite a bold bid by John Bowdler Music at Lingfield towards the end of the month, no further successes were recorded in February. The month-end figures of two wins from twenty-one runs produced a disappointing strike rate of 10.5%. Accordingly, the stable's overall percentage for the year fell to 20%. Win prize money had moved on to just £32,832. Given Johnston's reflective, self-critical nature, it comes as no surprise to learn that comparison of current results with past achievements is a feature of his organisation. Indeed, a result sheet, incorporating data on the two previous seasons, is printed out and circulated before each weekly management meeting.

Whilst many yards would have been satisfied with ten winners by the end of February, this represented the second-poorest start to a season for Johnston since 1993. Only in 1995 had fewer (eight) been achieved at the same stage. Part of the reason was, undoubtedly, a reduction in the number of runners. In 1996, 61 runners in January and February had yielded 13 winners. In 1997, 75 produced 19 whilst, the following year, 11 had been gained from 77. So far, in 1999, only 52 horses had run by the end of February. Asked to explain why, Johnston cited a number of reasons. Principal among them, and despite his yard's considerable success (between 1996 and 1998, he'd achieved 100 all-weather wins, at a strike-rate of 21%), was a growing disenchantment with British all-weather racing. So far as Johnston was concerned, he felt there was no rhyme or reason to race planning on the all-weather circuit; that prize money was derisory and that judging by the nature and frequency of injuries sustained by his horses in recent years, the racing surfaces themselves appeared to be deteriorating. In keeping with the growing trend of globalisation within racing, Johnston was therefore turning his thoughts towards winter alternatives to the British circuit. In particular, he is still looking at the possibility of racing more horses on snow in Switzerland and at the proposed new racecourse at Mijas on the Costa Del Sol. It is expected that all-weather racing will commence in the South of France at Cagnes-Sur-Mer and at Pau in the early part of 2000, with plans for an all-weather circuit at a major Paris track scheduled for completion in 2003. Speculation is also growing that British trainers may soon seek the opportunity of wintering horses in Dubai and Mark would hope to be in the vanguard of any such movement, not least because the yard already has a number of owners based there.

In the meantime, however, the races and money won in the opening couple of months of the year provided a launching pad from which the stable could push off at the start of the turf season on Town Moor.

March 1999

T o the flat racing aficionado the onset of March directs thoughts to Doncaster and the Lincoln meeting, even when the jumping brethren are in the midst of their preparations for Cheltenham. As Rudyard Kipling put it "No one thinks of winter when the grass is green!".

However, until Doncaster's watershed fixture commences, the all-weather game continues, and indeed its profile is raised somewhat as punters take an increasing interest in those horses who are being given a run on sand to prepare them for the turf season. In any event, the month of March started with another encouraging run from Thekryaati, albeit in defeat, when he failed by only a short head to regain the lead from Weet-A-Minute in a decent handicap over an extended nine furlongs at Wolverhampton on the 3rd. The following day saw Hormuz open the stable's monthly account at Lingfield, in the process giving apprentice Robbie Fitzpatrick his first win of the season for the stable.

After Thekryaati had run second again, at Lingfield on March 18th, it was decided to try him over a mile and a half in the opening race of the new turf season a week later. Runners on the all-weather were few and far between as the stable prepared for Doncaster. On the first day Thekryaati and Hormuz were declared, along with the smart White Heart (who looked to have a good chance in the Doncaster Mile) and Royal Rebel. Unfortunately, those fit from the all-weather disappointed, perhaps needing time to adjust to turf again. However, Royal Rebel, an uneasy favourite, managed a respectable third in the three-year-old maiden, whilst White Heart excelled when, under a confident ride from Darryll Holland, he prevailed in the first listed race of the season.

The same day, in Dubai, plans for a World Series of Racing sponsored by Emirates airline and comprising nine Championship races, each with a minimum value of $1 million, were revealed. British racing was to receive a boost by the inclusion of the King George VI and Queen Elizabeth Diamond Stakes at Ascot as the prestigious first leg. The aim of the Series was to produce "an equine World Champion" based on consistency over the series, points being awarded Formula 1 style to the first six home in each race. The other events in the schedule were the Breeders' Cup Turf, the Breeders' Cup Classic, the Esat Digifone Irish Champion Stakes at Leopardstown, Australia's BMW Cox Plate, the Canadian International at Woodbine, the Japan Cup, the Hong Kong Cup at Sha Tin, and the climactic Dubai World Cup at Nad Al Sheba in March 2000. Johnston was excited at the prospect of such a series but at such an early stage of the season it was impossible for him to know whether any of his charges would prove up to such fierce competition.

The stable's sole representative on Worthington Lincoln day was Kentucky Bullet in the closing seven-furlong handicap. Making his turf debut, the Housebuster colt proved a decisive winner for Joe Fanning at odds of 12-1. These domestic victories moved the win prize money total to £54,237, but the stable's thoughts had moved further afield. What's that proverb again? "March comes in like a lion and goes out like a lamb". Really?

Over in the United Arab Emirates preparations for the 1999 Dubai World Cup were being finalised. Although Johnston did not have a runner in the big race itself, his stable was represented at the meeting by the four-year-old Fruits of Love, long-time apple of his trainer's eye, and, indirectly, by Lend A Hand, the latter a successful juvenile under Johnston's tutelage before his absorption into the Godolphin empire. Johnston had been so impressed when inspecting Fruits of Love as a yearling at Goffs' 1996 Orby Yearling Sales that he went out on a limb to pay IR 75,000 gns for him, even though at that stage he didn't have an owner! Fruits of Love is a son of the American sire Hansel, himself a dual US classic winner in 1991 and subsequently an Eclipse Award winner. The horse performed with no little promise as a juvenile, winning a maiden at Newcastle comfortably before going down by two lengths to Bahr in listed company at Newbury. A fortnight later he ran Impressionist to a length in the Group 3 Futurity Stakes at the Curragh. On the basis of these promising runs, all during August, Timeform rated the colt at 102p in *Racehorses of 1997*. Shortly after the Futurity Stakes, however, he suffered a career-threatening injury, pulling up lame on the Middleham gallops in September 1997, though it took three months to have the problem diagnosed as a fractured ilium. To explain, a horse with a suspected fractured pelvis should not be moved in the first few months after the injury. As the appropriate equipment to effect the diagnosis could not be brought to the horse a formal diagnosis had to wait.

Mark's faith in the horse was not shaken despite the injury and the colt improved sufficiently as a three-year-old to win the Group 2 Princess of Wales's Stakes on Newmarket's July course. On dismounting, Michael Hills told Johnston that the horse would win the St Leger, the only problem being that the horse had not been entered, the race having closed some days before the running of this, one of the first recognised trials for Britain's oldest classic. This prompted Johnston to criticise the entry system for the Leger and for the classics in general in his weekly column in the *Racing Post*, the central thrust of his argument being that the present system of early-closing and forfeit stages often failed to attract the best horses, thus damaging the reputation and status of our top races. Given that prize money available in Britain compares most unfavourably with other major racing nations, he felt any further damage to reputation especially significant.

Fruits of Love had five more races. A rather disappointing third in the Group 3 Meld Stakes at the Curragh preceded a good fifth in the Group 2 Grand Prix de Deauville (beaten two and a half lengths by Epistolaire). He was then unplaced in the Group 3 Cumberland Lodge Stakes at Ascot, having failed to settle, before finishing fourth in the Group 2 Prix du Conseil de Paris at Longchamp. Called into the field late, he then proceeded to run a cracking race in the Hong Kong International Vase at Sha Tin, taking fifth behind Hong Kong's top colt Indigenous; at the end of the year these efforts resulted in a Timeform rating of 116 in the 1998 edition of *Racehorses*.

The racing programme marked out for Fruits of Love thus far in his career mirrors the attitude of Johnston to entries generally. Put simply, Johnston seeks to enter his horses where the return to the owner is maximised, both in terms of prize money and also in relation to the status of the races chosen. Value for money is high on his list of priorities, whether it be in assessing the price to which he is prepared to compete for a yearling at auction or in considering whether to supplement a horse for an early-closing race. Fruits of Love could have been supplemented to the Leger field for £20,000. However, even though owner Mick Doyle, who owns a super trawler and fish-processing plant in County Donegal, was happy to leave the final decision to his trainer, Johnston did not feel such a gamble was justified. A cause for regret, perhaps, in the light of the colt's subsequent achievements, but events in Dubai on March 28th were to erase any remaining vestiges of disappointment.

The fourth running of the Emirates Dubai World Cup was the centrepiece of the Nad Al Sheba card, but rich rewards were offered in the supporting races. Doyle was keen for Fruits of Love to run at the meeting, and the horse was duly entered in the £300,000 Dubai Turf Classic. At the owner's request, the ride was offered to Kieren Fallon.

The training challenge posed by running horses on a different continent is a substantial one; year in, year out, for example, Europeans gather more in hope than expectation to watch our heroes challenge North America's best thoroughbreds on their own patch in the Breeders' Cup . The small number of successful invaders tells its own story as to the magnitude of the task involved. Only an exceptional horse proves capable of winning.

Johnston has special memories of Nad Al Sheba on World Cup day. The intensity of interest in the horse and the sport for sport's sake, coupled with legendary Arab hospitality, imbued it with a distinctive, electric atmosphere. All this despite the absence of gambling, regarded by many elsewhere as racing's *raison d'être*. The richest race in the world and its supporting card have been developed to attract the cream of the crop from around the world. In particular, the rise in the number of North American participants bodes well for its further development, as does the inclusion of the principal race in the new World Series. It is not only the Maktoum family who know and appreciate their horses in Dubai. On this occasion a knowledgeable and enthusiastic crowd witnessed some exciting racing and close finishes, not least in the Turf Classic itself.

In addition to Fruits of Love, who went to post for the race substantially heavier than previously, having had only one 'proper' gallop since running in the Hong Kong International Vase, the field for the Dubai Turf Classic included a number of Group 1 winners. Notable among these were Godolphin's St Leger winner Nedawi, the mount of Frankie Dettori, and the top German horse Caitano, a multiple Group 1 winner who had been beaten only two and a half lengths into fifth in the 1998 Prix de l'Arc de Triomphe. Having half missed the kick when the starting stalls opened, Fallon was able to secure a place on the inside rail for most of the trip. In Fallon's words, it took a little time to get Fruits of Love balanced and the horse brought up the rear at the halfway stage. However, Fallon appeared to have found the key to riding 'Fruity', niggling away before producing him with a long, sustained run. Once asked for his effort, Fruits of Love surged through the pack to challenge four wide up the home straight and gradually wore down Nedawi to win by a neck. A superlative ride.

Although he has trained horses for Sheikh Mohammed, Sheikh Maktoum al Maktoum and other members of the Maktoum family, Johnston was uncertain as to how his hosts would react to the defeat of their St Leger winner. He need not have worried. The first person to greet Fruits of Love as he returned from the track to the winner's enclosure was Sheikh Rashid, son of Sheikh Mohammed and a keen and knowledgeable follower of racing. Echoing the trainer's own thoughts, he proclaimed to the winning connections "I knew this was a good horse". His father was equally impressed, and Johnston recalls that he was left in no doubt that Sheikh Mohammed himself was genuinely delighted by his success. Effusive in his congratulations, he posed happily for photographers with the winning connections and showed no sign of disappointment whatsoever that his own runners had been eclipsed.

In terms of prize money this success provided Johnston with the second-biggest win of his career to date. Although the race does not yet enjoy pattern status, in winning Fruits of Love had defeated proven Group 1 performers. Thus plans were made to aim him at the Irish St Leger, the feeling being that the horse would be suited by the additional two furlongs of the Curragh race. The success was special to Johnston for a number of reasons. Firstly, it represented his first winner as a trainer outside Europe. For someone prepared to travel any distance in pursuit of winners and whose ambition and goal-setting knows few bounds, success on a global scale was particularly sweet. Secondly, Johnston was delighted that long-time owner Mick Doyle should have enjoyed such a red-letter day, both in terms of kudos and hard cash, particularly in light of what would now appear to have been that 'missed' opportunity of the Leger. Doyle recalls that "when I joined up with Mark he had ten horses. Now he is well into three figures. That says a lot." Thirdly, Johnston was especially delighted that Fruits of Love should have fulfilled the potential he first spotted at Goffs in 1996.

When questioned about the race, Johnston claimed little of the credit. The fact that the horse had had only one proper gallop and was "heavier than we wanted" was dismissed as being not entirely deliberate. Ironically, Johnston recalls that in the days prior to the race, whilst some of the contenders were impressive on the track in their work, he was almost embarrassed by Fruits of Love who was just "hacking along looking desperately slow". The key to Fruits of Love's success might have been his freshness: plus the trainer's gut feeling that the colt was ready to fire.

The final race on a memorable night, the Nad Al Sheba Mile, run on dirt, was taken by former Kingsley House inmate Lend a Hand.

Johnston remains effusive in his praise for the Maktoum family's support of racing, both in Dubai and around the world. Their vast investment in the bloodstock has significantly improved the quality of European racing. The prize money won by Fruits of Love in the Turf Classic was more than three times that gained at Newmarket. Money is hugely important to Johnston in his strategic planning. As success has snowballed over the last few years, so the quality of yearlings purchased on behalf of his owners has improved, largely because they have been willing to reinvest winnings. Johnston takes great satisfaction out of this 'partnership' which he has worked hard to forge, and there is little doubt that he has the owners' interests at heart whenever important decisions have to be made. The euphoria of Fruits of Love's victory, following on the heels of White Heart's Doncaster win, ensured the yard looked forward to the new turf season with renewed optimism and vigour.

The monthly strike rate for March ended at 4 winners from 26 runners, or 15.4%. The rate for the year to date moved to 17.9%. However, the most important figure of the month was the pot of £154,652 won by the fruits of 'Fruity's' labours in the desert!

CHAPTER SEVEN

April 1999

D reams of further success for Fruits of Love, perhaps even a Group 1 victory, were rudely interrupted on Britain's motorway network on the evening of April 1st. Having travelled back by air to the UK from Dubai, Fruits of Love was being transported by horsebox back to Middleham when potential disaster struck just after the box turned off the M25 onto the M1 north. In addition to the driver, also travelling were Robynne Watton, and Fruits of Love's own lass, Gail Alderson. Johnston, who was travelling home by car to Middleham at the time, recalls that at about 6.30 pm he received a call from Brendan Holland, the Head Lad, to the effect that Robynne had rung to say that for some reason the horse had gone berserk and was trying to climb over the partition in the box. Johnston recalls saying to Robynne when she herself came on the phone "can't you get hold of his head" at the same time hearing shouting, banging and thrashing about in the background. He remembers Robynne saying "it's coming over", and before long the horse had indeed managed somehow to get over the partition, as a result of which he was lying upside down in the groom's passageway in front of the stalls. Robynne was clearly close to tears and Johnston remembers telling her to calm down, reassuring her that there was nothing more she could do at that time.

Robynne recalls the incident vividly. "We'd been going for about half an hour. Fruits of Love had been standing quietly, picking at his haynet. Gail had been sat with him and then came through and joined us. Soon after, we just heard a thud. Gail looked through and shouted "he's over". So we stopped the box and went through. He'd got his legs half over the partition, just up to his knees, so I thought we'd be able to push him back. Well, no, no we couldn't get him over at all. The more we pushed the more he wanted to come out. Then, eventually, he just seemed to scramble his way forward over the top. His head went down into the corner and he just gently slid over till he was wedged upside down, and that's where he lay for half an hour until we got to the vets college. I didn't think he'd come out alive."

Robynne asked Brendan whether she should phone the fire brigade for assistance, and an emergency 999 call was duly made. Meantime, back at Kingsley House, Brendan Holland was on the phone simultaneously to Robynne in the box, to the transport company who owned it and to Mark on his mobile phone whilst the drama unfolded. Although distraught and frustrated by his inability to assist further, Johnston managed to think rationally, and he urged Brendan to try and find a good horse vet as a matter of urgency. Anyone involved in the racing industry is only too aware of the vicissitudes of working with thoroughbreds and the myriad of problems and disappointments which these fragile animals can bring. Even so, one can only imagine Johnston's feelings upon learning that the new star in the Kingsley House firmament might be about to be extinguished in such a bizarre and horrific manner.

Fortunately, the driver realised that they were not far from the Royal Veterinary College at Potters Bar and an instant decision was made to go there. A frantic journey followed, with the driver, Robynne and Gail travelling in the cab whilst Fruits of Love was stranded on his back effectively lying across the area immediately to the rear of them.

Johnston urged Brendan by telephone to ensure that the vet school was fully briefed and knew exactly what was coming to them, both in terms of the nature of the problem and the value of the horse. A police escort was requested but did not materialise, although in fairness it transpired that the journey took only around 30 minutes. When the box arrived at the college it was met by a team of three veterinary surgeons, a veterinary nurse and by three appliances from White Watch at Potters Bar Fire Station under sub-officer Martin Graham. The fire appliances are recorded as having set out from Potters Bar at 7.22 pm.

When the side door of the box was removed, Martin Graham saw that the horse was trapped in a tiny space, covered in sweat and with his head thrashing against the back of the driver's compartment.

There is an old saying "cometh the hour, cometh the man", but in this case the heroine of the hour proved to be vet Sarah Freeman, 27. Faced with a horse wedged on his back in a state of severe shock, she managed to manoeuvre herself fearlessly into a position sitting between his legs. From there she was able to attach a catheter into the horse's jugular vein and administered a sedative to prevent the horse becoming dehydrated. "The cramped position he was in was our worst nightmare" she recalls. "You need room to work. They were so lucky the horse did not smash through into the cab, because he could easily have ended up on the driver's seat." At this point, Robynne called Johnston to report that they had reached the college, that the horse had been sedated and that they were sending for a winch to lift him out of his predicament. Johnston then realised that the horse was in good hands and that by continuing to talk on the phone he might simply be interfering with the rescue operation. He asked his staff to let him know once the situation had been resolved.

The firefighters marvelled at the bravery of Sarah. Martin Graham describes the scene. "There was this tiny girl, brave as a lion, sitting astride his back trying to fit the catheter. Then he would start thrashing around and we would pull her to safety, but she insisted on going back. I've never seen anything like it." Leading fireman Tony Ludlow remembers that at times Fruits of Love was "like a bucking bronco" and he too was in awe of Sarah's actions.

Possibly as a result of his veterinary training, Johnston was cool and analytical in the face of this crisis. In fact, as the drama unfolded outside his control his immediate thoughts were that the horse was underinsured, having regard to its recent triumph! He also recalls concluding that if "Fruity's" life could be saved the horse had probably not done enough to make himself commercially viable as a sire. If only the Turf Classic had been a Group race!

Meanwhile, the dramatic rescue was continuing apace and the fortune of the incident having occurred relatively close to such an appropriate establishment was about to become clear. The college's Sefton Equine Hospital, named after the horse which survived the Hyde Park bombing in 1982, was particularly well equipped to deal with an emergency of this nature. The operating theatres at the college include an overhead rail which leads to a loading bay, the normal purpose of which is to assist in the removal of carcasses, or as Alastair Down in the *Racing Post* so aptly described it "the knacker's rail usually used to remove from that establishment horses who haven't made it through the night". The fire brigade and the college staff were ingenious enough to use this system in reverse once Fruits of Love had been anaesthetised. After he'd had lost consciousness, the firemen began to attempt to remove the partition trapping him, working carefully with an electrical saw. Eventually, his weight forced the panel out and the firemen dived for cover as hooves lashed out momentarily once free. One of the vets then placed a hobble on his legs and Fruits of Love was eventually dragged onto a salvage sheet from the horsebox, down the loading ramp and attached by the hobbles to the rail which would take him to the operating theatre.

The medical team comprising Freeman, Dr Eddie Cauvin, and Dylan Gorvy feared that the horse might have broken a bone in his back or pelvis, and it was clear that he had been severely shocked by the incident. Fortunately, and incredibly, it transpired that he'd escaped without serious injury and, when hoisted from the theatre and in a padded recovery cell, Sarah Freeman administered another sedative before leaving him to come round. By this stage the veterinary staff's major concern was that Fruits of Love would not have a bad recovery from the anaesthetic, as a horse which has been trapped often panics when waking.

At 7.55 pm Johnston received the phone call he had been worried might never come, to the effect that the horse had come through his ordeal, was in the recovery room and that his prospects for recovery were good. Mark could hardly believe that in spite of such an ordeal the colt had escaped major injury, sustaining only bruising and cuts to an eye which required a few stitches. Sarah Freeman recalls that this fortunate outcome was assisted by Fruits of Love himself, who, when he came round from the anaesthetic, didn't panic and was "very quiet and very sensible"; in every way a model patient. 'Fruity' soon climbed to his feet and began moving around, and within an hour had exchanged his padded cell for a normal stable. In less than forty-eight hours he was on his way home to Middleham.

It remained to be seen, however, whether this dramatic episode would leave a mental scar; perhaps all of his luck had been used up in surviving the scare. As is so often the case in racing, time alone would tell…

After such a dramatic start to the month one couldn't help wondering what the rest of April would have in store. Comparison of figures for the first quarter of 1998 showed that by the end of March in each year the fourteen-winner mark had been reached. This year's strike rate was slightly better and, of course, Fruits of Love's lucrative success had guaranteed a significant advantage in terms of prize money won. However, the year's start could not be regarded as a vintage one by Johnston's own high standards. In 1996, 17 winners had been registered in the equivalent period; in 1994, Mister Baileys' year, 24 had been achieved, and in 1997 no fewer than 28 winners had been on the board by the beginning of April (at a superior strike rate too!). So, although stable spirits were high after Dubai, the team was in no doubt that much hard work lay ahead if it was to build successfully on the foundations of its early-season campaign.

As is inevitable given the timing of the first four British classics (which to yours truly seems ludicrously early in this day and age), no sooner is Doncaster's curtain-raising fixture over than thoughts turn towards Newmarket's Craven meeting, the classic trials and the Guineas meeting itself. Indeed, Kempton Park's Guineas trials, the Easter Stakes and the Masaka Stakes, were run as early as April 3rd in 1999.

In 1998 Johnston had a live contender for the 2000 Guineas in Lend A Hand, a Great Commotion colt who had won all his starts as a two-year-old bar his debut. Having been a runaway winner of the Gran Criterium in Milan on his final appearance at two, it was initially planned that he should contest the Italian 2000 Guineas but a decision to switch to Newmarket paid off. Like Mister Baileys, Lend A Hand was sent to Newmarket without a preparatory race, starting third favourite behind French hotpot Xaar and the Irish-trained King of Kings. Lend A Hand performed with great credit, battling on to take a well-deserved second place behind the latter. He later joined the Godolphin operation, as has already been mentioned, and was opening his account for them when lifting the Nad Al Sheba Mile.

At the outset of April 1999 the Middleham stable did not appear to hold any likely stars for the Guineas' meeting, but hopes in general were raised significantly on Easter Monday at Newcastle when the stable secured a treble, the experienced Tiler's win in a competitive seven-furlong handicap being followed by maiden-race wins for Royal Rebel, over a mile, and Doonaree, over an extended mile and a half. The manner of Doonaree's win was most impressive, and given his breeding (his dam was an Italian Guineas winner and his sire has carried all before him at stud) plus his price tag (he cost IR 200,000 gns as a yearling), a bright future was now being anticipated.

Following in Fruits of Love's footsteps in flying the flag for Johnston abroad during the month were Gaelic Storm, a tough gelding by Shavian and David Abell's three-year-old Polar Falcon colt, Ice. The former travelled to the Curragh for the Group 3 Gladness Stakes over seven furlongs, attempting to step up into pattern company after an excellent campaign as a four-year-old in handicaps. He ran well to finish one and a half lengths second to Dermot Weld's rather in and out colt Two-Twenty-Two, who was enjoying one of his better days. However, in Dielsdorf, Switzerland, Ice ran out a convincing winner of the Grand Prix Graff Capital Management (Swiss 2000 Guineas) under Kieren Fallon.

And so to the Craven meeting at Newmarket, where the stable's intended representative in the fillies' classic, Atlantic Destiny, put her claims on the line in one of the traditional trials, the Group 3 Nell Gwyn Stakes on April 13th. Due to ongoing building work on the Rowley Mile course, all Newmarket fixtures for the season were transferred to the July course, a move which proved controversial at various points, notably concerning deteriorating going and the effect of the draw. Johnston was concerned that Atlantic Destiny's temperament, which he described as "hyper-excitable", might get the better of her and so formed a plan to try and calm her down. Step forward thirteen-year-old Ian Smith of Fleets Farm, Middleham, who agreed to lend Bam Bam, a Suffolk Cross ewe, to Kingsley House to act as Atlantic Destiny's travelling companion and soulmate. A more relaxed Atlantic Destiny went amenably and early to post and, once under way, Darryll Holland made every effort to settle her in the early stages. However, the filly was a little squeezed for room at a vital stage, in the circumstances running well enough for fifth, a performance which her trainer described as "neither startling, nor a desperate disappointment". Given that Bam Bam seemed to be having a beneficial effect on Atlantic Destiny, the two proving inseparable, Johnston decided after some thought to let her take her chance in the 1000 Guineas. It should be said that the stable staff required a period of adjustment in learning to deal with Bam Bam's sophisticated palate, and when it was mentioned at a weekly management meeting that she was being offered the same feed as her equine companion Johnston quickly pointed out that this was entirely inappropriate and could even be life-threatening to the poor beast!

The first blow for the two-year-old members of the team was struck by the Soviet Lad colt Hammer And Sickle in a maiden race at Ripon on the 15th. On the same afternoon a three-year-old colt by Robellino called Tonic was victorious on his seasonal debut in the mile maiden race on the same card. Both winners were ridden by Darryll Holland and as John McCririck, often unfairly critical of trainer columns, will doubtless have noted, both were strongly tipped by Mark Johnston in a *Racing Post* stable tour feature published that day. Their starting prices were 15/2 and 5/1 respectively!

The Thirsk Classic Trial on April 17th was won by the stable's Tissifer in some style under a strong ride from John Carroll. The Polish Precedent colt had disappointed his trainer somewhat when, after promising wins at Epsom and Kempton Park, he'd failed to progress on his final start as a two-year-old in the Group 3 Beresford Stakes at the Curragh. However, all was forgiven after Thirsk and connections were now considering sending him for the German equivalent of the 2000 Guineas, the Mehl-Mulhens-Rennen (Group 2), at Cologne in the middle of May.

The following day Johnston ran two of the yard's leading three-year-olds abroad. Firstly, Royal Rebel confirmed the promise of his Newcastle win when finishing only a neck behind Aidan O'Brien's useful Generous colt Cupid in Leopardstown's listed Ballysax Stakes over ten furlongs. A crack at one of the Derby trials was now on his agenda. Secondly, the Environment Friend filly, Three Green Leaves, successful no fewer than five times as a two-year-old, made her seasonal debut in the Italian 1000 Guineas at Rome, the Premio Regina Elena (Group 2). However, she disappointed badly, finishing only fourteenth of sixteen, her performance being attributed to the heavy ground.

Doonaree's eagerly awaited return to the track came at Catterick on the 21st in a four-runner conditions race, this time over a distance just short of one and a half miles. Barry Hills's useful colt Toto Caelo provided the only serious opposition but couldn't extend Doonaree in any way, Darryll Holland being able to direct all of his efforts to restricting the winning margin to just one length! A step up in class seemed more than justified. Perhaps inevitably, the question of Doonaree's possible participation in the Derby arose. However, Johnston revealed that the colt had been taken out of the race at the previous forfeit stage. In something of a reprise of remarks made after Fruits of Love's win at Newmarket as a three-year-old, he went on to roundly criticise the entry system for the race, leading to a headline in the *Racing Post* on April 23rd of "Johnston slams Derby system". Mark actually pointed out that the present system fails to attract the best horses.

Specifically, Johnston criticised the early entry stage and the total amount of money owners were required to pay for the run (£6,250 in 1999, a supplementary entry costing £75,000). "The entries should be made later and cost less. Then the best horses would run. How are owners meant to know what trip or ground their horses are going to need as yearlings?" Picking up on his recent positive experience in Dubai he added: "We have just run Fruits of Love in Dubai and it cost us nothing. In Britain we're living in the past".

Hard on the heels of Johnston's comments a bizarre brush with officialdom followed after the running of Evesham, a Sheikh Mohammed-owned colt by Septieme Ciel, in Division I of the Redmile Maiden Stakes at Leicester on April 24th. Johnston was eventually fined £400 for making a double declaration. Five days earlier he had entered the colt in maiden races at Ripon and Leicester on the same afternoon but, on seeing the entries, had a clear preference for Ripon. Three days beforehand it came to his notice that Ripon was in some doubt, due to water lying on the track. Accordingly, Johnston telephoned the course to be advised that no inspection was planned. Shortly afterwards, Johnston learned to his dismay that not only was an inspection now scheduled at Ripon for Friday morning, the day prior to the race, but that one was also to be held at Leicester on the same morning!

Leicester's was held first after which it was decided that racing could go ahead. Ripon, on the other hand, decided to have a further inspection the following morning. Johnston sought the advice of the Clerk of the Course at Ripon, who frankly admitted that the course was unraceable at that time but that prospects might improve if no further rain materialised. He was advised that the safer bet was to go to Leicester and duly declared Evesham there.

The situation was then complicated further when Ripon's race was re-opened, having attracted only one declared runner. Naturally, Johnston wished to reinstate Evesham, and decided to consult Weatherbys, who in turn consulted the Race Planning Department of the British Horseracing Board. The rules don't allow such a double declaration but, given the weather and circumstances, common sense surely suggested that little harm would be done if Johnston went ahead and declared for both. The advice he received was to do so although he also acknowledged that it was pointed out that a fine might be levied. As a matter of courtesy Johnston advised the press that the colt would only run at Leicester if Ripon didn't take place.

In the event, Ripon was abandoned, Evesham ran at Leicester and Johnston was duly fined, £400. That sum was subsequently reduced to £275 while Johnston was considering an appeal. He decided not to press the matter further when reminded that a £300 deposit would require to be lodged (and perhaps forfeited) for one to take place. Effectively Mark was fined for failing to run his horse in a race which did not take place! As they say, "rules are for the guidance of wise men and the obedience of fools"!

Heir apparent to Double Trigger's staying crown was Spirit of Love, a four-year-old chestnut colt by Trempolino, who had been virtually unchallenged when winning the previous year's Cesarewitch at Newmarket. Beforehand, comparisons with the great horse were clearly premature as, on handicap ratings alone, had Double Trigger been entered for that race he would have been required to concede 1 st 10 lb to Spirit of Love, together with a further 11 lb weight-for-age. That said, hopes were high that Spirit of Love would progress to the top of the stayers' division. In line with these lofty aspirations, Spirit of Love's campaign was the tried and tested 'Trigger trail' of the Sagaro Stakes, Henry II Stakes and Ascot Gold Cup. In the Sagaro he went off 4/1 favourite. However, having attempted to make all, he ran alarmingly wide on the home turn before keeping on well to finish fourth, four and a quarter lengths behind the John Dunlop-trained Celeric. Once headed, the horse had been tenderly handled by Darryll Holland and as Mark Johnston observed: "This run showed us that he is up to the class. There is room for improvement all round but, then again, he doesn't need to improve that much either. He was coming back again at the finish after they sprinted past him on the bend. I wasn't disappointed with him and another half mile in the Gold Cup will make a huge difference." As the colt had had foot problems and would come on for the race this seemed a reasonably conservative appraisal of his future prospects and the rest of his plans remained unaltered.

As April drew to a close the four-year-old filly Rafting landed a mile-and-a-half handicap at Musselburgh on the 30th, bringing the monthly winners' total to 9. Win prize money totals had moved on to £92,524 (Britain) and £160,602 (abroad). The strike rate for the month was 13.6%, slightly down on the same month in 1998. For the year to date, the rate had slipped to a disappointing 15.97%. The number of winners in Britain for 1999 now stood at 21.

CHAPTER EIGHT

May 1999

E ven the most cursory analysis of the Kingsley House operation shows that the beginning of May appears to mark a watershed, after which the number of winners suddenly multiplies. Take, for example, 1995 when only fourteen had been attained by the end of April. The next month no fewer than sixteen horses obliged. Again, in 1997, a disappointing trickle of four winners in April preceded a comparative torrent (fifteen) the following month.

Johnston reckons the main reason for such a trend is due to the High Moor gallops, which usually open early in May. Instead of a fairly short walk up Kirkgate, a right turn past Middleham Castle and on to the Low Moor for exercise, his string now faces a much longer and more challenging uphill walk, right across the Low Moor and on further uphill to the gathering point for High Moor exercise. The High Moor gallops themselves are more demanding and its all-weather strip, one and a half miles long, has a different surface to that of the seven-furlong one on the Low Moor. After work, the horses seem to enjoy the comparatively long walk back to the yard. In simple terms, they work harder and enjoy a little more variety in their regimes. Who knows, they may even benefit from the fabulous views from the vantage point of the High Moor? If you haven't been, it's well worth a visit!

The horses under Johnston's care enjoy facilities out of the top drawer. When Mark Johnston Racing Limited acquired Kingsley House only thirty-four boxes were available and the yard was in a rundown condition. Now it boasts sixty-seven, with an on-site equine swimming pool, electronic horse walkers and lunging rings. Kingsley House also has some of the very best veterinary facilities, including a veterinary room with endoscopy and x-ray facilities. A separate weighing room is available. When Warwick House was bought in 1994 an electronic horse walker was also installed. As a matter of routine, and in addition to exercise on the gallops, the horses can be given spells on one of the walkers or sent swimming. An ongoing programme of staff training in the proper use of the swimming pool is designed to ensure that there are plenty of staff members able and willing to supervise such activity. Johnston is also actively seeking to acquire a further yard, with facilities for turning out horses, to complement what he already has at his disposal.

As May got under way the memory of Fruits of Love's win was beginning to fade and Johnston began to feel some concern about the results and the condition of some of the horses. The High Moor was not yet open. How would the month pan out? Would the past trend of an acceleration of the rate of success in May manifest itself again? In the meantime, Mark's attention was distracted by the publication in the *Racing Post* of an article in which Tony Morris and John Randall attempted to classify past winners of the 2000 Guineas. Johnston was appalled to note that Mister Baileys had been classified as a "poor" winner of the Guineas, and couldn't resist writing about his feelings when his regular column in the paper returned on Saturday May 1st (ironically Guineas day!). He stated that comparisons between different generations are well-nigh impossible and felt, at the least, that he had more concrete evidence available to him as to the relative merit of the horse than would have been available to the authors. Incidentally, that article is part of a book by the same authors entitled *A Century of Champions,* available from the same publishers as this tome!

Johnston's weekly column in the Post represents a significant commitment of time and effort on his part. His schedules show a man who usually rises some time before 6 am in order to supervise the first of three or four lots and who then, most days from March to November, travels to a racecourse. A trip to a southern track, or worse still an evening meeting at, say Hamilton or Ayr, will mean a return to base very late in the day, with the prospect of having to compile the following morning's work list before being able to relax. Little wonder Mark has mastered the art of catching up on sleep in the car; Philip Marrison takes care of the driving!

When not racing, morning exercise normally finishes around noon, after which Johnston's time is taken up in all sorts of ways. For instance, he might be meeting visitors, returning calls to owners or their managers, dealing with the press, reviewing the vet diary, looking at specific horses which have come to his attention (either from reviewing the diary or in conversation with the staff), liaising with BHB handicappers, catching up on correspondence or dealing with the 'commercial' side of the business and its associated paper-work. If he is lucky, he may find time for some lunch before evening stables. From my observation of Tuesday morning meetings, it is clear he spends long hours looking at his horses in their boxes. In addition to its more technical and medical aspects the vet diary contains a computer print out of comments made about the horses by Susanna Ballinger and other senior members of staff on a daily basis and, in chairing the meeting, Mark will frequently pick up on these, querying them in a manner which displays a detailed knowledge of the cut, bruise, filling, chafe or other condition in question.

In addition to the horses in his care and the physical demands of his profession, he is also the father of two schoolchildren with whom he attempts to interact and share activities as much as possible. Thus a commitment to write 1200 words per week in a form ready to be published in a national newspaper is not something to be undertaken lightly. Often, Johnston will compose his copy in the late evening or early hours of the morning after preparing the work list. He relishes the opportunity of expressing his views on racing's matters of the moment and over the years has been more than willing to grasp the nettle and expound his views on controversial issues such as the whip, jockeys' overweight and the apparent decline of the Derby. Sometimes he has had numerous topics about which he wished to write and found the task comparatively easy. At others, he will struggle to fill his column, but his work is often informative, usually entertaining and even (sometimes) funny! Johnston's views frequently provoke letters from readers which are less than complimentary. A Mr Smith from Dublin accused him of arrogance in the context of a piece he'd written in defence of the proper use of whips. Champion jockey Kieren Fallon also saw fit to write to the *Racing Post* in protest at an article in which Johnston questioned the profes-sionalism of jockeys who accepted rides at low weights only to prove unable to ride at those on the specified day.

Deirdre Johnston does not enjoy the criticism levelled at her husband for expressing his views, particularly when responses resort to vitriolic and personal abuse. She questions whether the angst caused on such occasions outweighs the advantages of writing the column. Mark also feels that the *Racing Post*'s editorial staff are happier when he confines the subject matter of his column to a discussion of the wellbeing of his horses, but he reserves the right to air his opinions as he sees fit. So far as yours truly is concerned, informed comment is a welcome addition to any racing debate. Without intending to criticise other pillars of the training profession, do members of the racing public really know where Henry Cecil stands on the use of the whip or what Luca Cumani feels about the vagaries of the fixture list? Do we know if Sir Michael Stoute regards the inaugural Shergar Cup, named after his outstanding 1981 Derby winner, as a success or failure and whether Richard Hannon supports a rise in the minimum weights? Wouldn't it be interesting to find out?

The first runner in May was Evesham in the Spring Maiden Stakes at Thirsk, ridden by Pierre Strydom, the South African champion jockey, for whom Mark had agreed to provide accommodation and some rides during a six-week educational stint in Britain. The pair finished fourth of ten. Later that afternoon Strydom rode a winner for William Haggas' Newmarket yard on Picture Puzzle. The following day saw the first fillies' classic, the Sagitta 1000 Guineas Stakes run at Newmarket. With Darryll Holland opting to ride John Gosden's Capistrano Day, Johnston offered Strydom the ride on Atlantic Destiny and the filly ran well enough to finish eleventh of the twenty-two runners. However a return to sprinting seemed the logical next move for Bam Bam's buddy.

On the same card, Strydom rode David Abell's Night Shift colt Alberich in a competitive mile and a half handicap. Attempting to make all, the colt was passed by Her Majesty The Queen's Blueprint, ridden by Frankie Dettori, two furlongs from home but kept on well for second. Johnston had noticed already that the South African appeared to be losing his place in races; he wondered whether he was "taking a pull" and suggested that he had even done this during his winning ride for William Haggas. He resolved to raise the matter with him, but no satisfactory explanation was forthcoming from Pierre.

At Doncaster the following day, Darryll Holland rode the speedy two-year-old colt Hammer And Sickle to victory in the Wiseton Novice Auction Stakes, only to be disqualified. Drawn in stall 3, Holland had come across sharply to the rails and the stewards took the view that in carrying out this manoeuvre he had interfered with some of the horses drawn on his inside. A six-day suspension was imposed on the rider, who was to be beset by such problems as the season unfolded. The all-weather performer Thekryaati ran an encouraging race in a useful handicap later that afternoon but, as Chester's May meeting loomed, the stable was still looking for its first winner of the month.

Doonaree's disappointing performance in the Victor Chandler Chester Vase has already been discussed, but the Chester meeting did yield a success, in fact the second of the month, when Harryana, a two-year-old filly by Efisio, took the EBF Sefton Maiden Stakes from Peter Chapple-Hyam's Shining Hour. Harryana had been unlucky not to score on her debut at Hamilton at the end of March, Joe Fanning having nursed her home in heavy conditions only to lose out close home to a harder-ridden winner. This time Darryll Holland was in the saddle and she saw her race out thoroughly.

The first winner of the month had been achieved some ten minutes earlier at Southwell when Robbie Fitzpatrick drove John Bowdler Music ahead in the final furlong of the six-furlong seller. However, Paul Dean's four-year-old Soviet Star gelding was sold for 8,300 gns at the subsequent auction.

Pierre Strydom also got in on the winning act when producing Star Rage two furlongs from home to win a competitive Beverley handicap over an extended two miles on May 8th. Now nine, this was David Abell's valiant gelding's sixteenth career win.

On the same day the inaugural Blue Square Shergar Cup, designed as a team event between Europe and the Middle East, took place at Goodwood and drew a high-class turnout. The inspiration of BHB Chairman Peter Savill, it represented an attempt to introduce a team championship to racing, the sides captained by Robert Sangster and Sheikh Mohammed respectively. As things turned out, the event received a very mixed reception. On the positive side, its organisers could fairly claim that it was the first race meeting to be staged in Europe with a minimum race value of £50,000; that all prize money was raised without any call being made on the Levy Board for funding; that race entry was free to owners and racecourse entry free to all stable lads and lasses throughout the country; that owners and trainers were to be given free entry and enjoy free hospitality and that participants from Ireland, France and Germany had been attracted. Savill argued further that, judged on ratings, the quality of the six races was equivalent to two Group 1s, a Group 2, two Group 3s and a listed race.

On the negative side, critics argued that the growing internationalisation of racing militated against the whole concept of the event; that it was difficult for the public to relate to the teams; that Lingfield's Derby trial fixture was adversely and unfairly affected by the competition; that the cost of admission badges was unjustifiably high and that the promoters, Mark McCormack's International Management Group (IMG), had insufficient expertise and experience in staging and managing major race meetings.

On the whole, Johnston welcomed the initiative, regarding it as "a completely new concept for British racing which will surely stimulate interest in our sport". Especially because of the prize money on offer, Johnston was keen to support the event, and he declared White Heart and Princely Heir, both owned by Sheikh Maktoum al Maktoum, to run on behalf of the Middle Eastern team. White Heart ran moderately, but although Princely Heir finished second-last in his race, his was a more encouraging effort. The Fairy King colt, winner of a Group 1 race as a two-year-old, ran up with the pace for a long way in a strongly-run affair over a distance of almost ten furlongs, way beyond his best. The Cup went to the European team, who snatched victory from the jaws of defeat in the final race. Despite all the reservations expressed, Johnston's view was that the exercise had been worthwhile. Paul Haigh wrote an excellent piece in the *Racing Post* on the day of the Cup in which he summarised the arguments for and against in his own inimitable style. He concluded, on balance, that the event was worthy of support "because it is an innovation and racing needs innovations if it is to extend its audience to that benighted 90% of the population who still dwell beyond its thrall".

Although Peter Savill's energies were focused at Goodwood, at least a part of his attention must have strayed to Lingfield Park where he was represented by two of Johnston's inmates, Royal Rebel in the Pertemps Derby Trial Stakes and Acicula in the Tote Sprint Stakes, a valuable handicap. With Mark at Goodwood to saddle the Maktoum horses (and no doubt to partake of the free hospitality!), Deirdre represented the stable at Lingfield in company with her elder son, Charlie, already as sharp and enterprising as his father. Much to Charlie's delight he was interviewed on Channel 4 Racing, and when asked to comment on Royal Rebel's prospects, he refused to dismiss the horse's chances despite the odds available of 25/1. So well did he deal with John Francome's interview that Jim McGrath's ad-lib at the end of the interview was to the effect that he had obviously inherited some of his father's confidence! The Channel 4 team was fortunate Charlie didn't attempt to sell the produce of the chickens he keeps at home. Not for nothing is he known as the Middleham egg magnate! He's clearly no bad judge either, as Royal Rebel seemed to relish the longer trip, finishing third, only half a length behind the Aga Khan's Daliapour, at that time strongly fancied for the Derby itself. Royal Rebel also finished five lengths clear of the fourth horse, Fantastic Light, with whom he had endured a barging match early in the straight. Prior to the race Johnston regarded the colt as mentally immature and inexperienced but now, assuming normal progress, began to think in terms of a Group 1 or 2 race for him. Acicula also ran with great credit, finishing fourth of twenty in the sprint, first home of those drawn low. Her performance represented a useful seasonal debut by any standards.

Dante Stakes day at York saw Johnston introduce a well-bred two-year-old colt named Dramatic Quest (by Zafonic, out of a half sister to the Arc winner Suave Dancer) in a six-furlong conditions race. The only runner with no previous experience, he was at a major disadvantage in such unusual surroundings. To reach the course horses have to endure a long walk from the stables across the Knavesmire to the pre-parade ring. Bearing that in mind, Dramatic Quest was far from disgraced, racing prominently until two furlongs from home. His name must have been jotted in many a notebook afterwards!

On Thursday May 13th, the final day of York's spring fixture, Ice, despite top weight, followed up his Swiss success in the concluding handicap over a mile. Earlier in the day Yavana's Pace, a seven-year-old gelding, who had performed with such consistency and success in 1998 (his campaign ended with a win in the November Handicap under 9 st 10 lb) made his seasonal debut in the Merewood Homes Yorkshire Cup (Group 2) over a distance just short of fourteen furlongs. What's more, he ran a cracker to finish fourth to Richard Hannon's Churlish Charm and it seemed reasonable to assume he would come on for the race.

Just seven days after her Lingfield exertions Acicula was turned out in the Coral Sprint Handicap at Newmarket. She was strongly supported, starting second favourite at 4/1 but, unfortunately, ran disappointingly, beaten over eight lengths behind Mitcham. On the same card, Atlantic Destiny finished fourth of eight in a listed fillies' stakes over six furlongs, this time keeping on as though a longer trip might suit her after all.

On Sunday May 16th Tissifer lined up for the Mehl-Mulhens-Rennen (German 2000 Guineas) at Cologne. Britain was also represented by Bahamian Bandit and Berlioz, though in the event none of the home-trained horses figured prominently as odds-on favourite and unbeaten German horse, Sumitas, comfortably landed the spoils. Tissifer ran no sort of race, finishing tailed-off last. Johnston was later to write that, having checked Tissifer thoroughly, he could ascertain no apparent reason for him to have run so badly. He pointed out that he felt he dare not speculate about the reasons for fear of falling foul of Jockey Club Instruction H14, which states that a trainer must report anything which might have adversely affected a horse's performance. Effectively this is a rule which can encourage trainers to be less frank in dealing with enquiries about their horses, argues Johnston.

Bearing in mind Johnston's emerging concern about results at the beginning of the month and comparing them with past trends, there's no doubt he was bitterly disappointed by the performance of the stable's runners during the first half of the month. The early potential shown by

Doonaree and Tissifer hadn't been realised. White Heart had failed to build upon his Doncaster win, and even though Yavana's Pace, Spirit of Love and Royal Rebel had all performed with some credit the fact remained that by the middle of the month only four winners had been achieved.

Johnston had voiced his concerns to the staff at the weekly meeting on May 4th, but, as the High Moor gallops had not yet been opened, the point wasn't unduly laboured. However further concern was expressed on May 11th when it fell to Brendan Holland, the Head Lad, to comment on results, always the first item on the agenda. By the following Tuesday, and with no further winners having been achieved, Johnston's patience was wearing thin. A major inquest was held. Johnston described the statistics as "very bad, horrendous even" and invited his team to suggest why this was so and what they felt could be done to improve matters. It was put forward that the delay in opening the High Moor was the principal problem. Johnston concurred that the opening of those gallops had usually heralded an immediate difference in results but felt that this was not the only source of difficulty. Instead, he focused on the horses' weights and feeding regime, the overall principle being to feed (four times a day) and work a lot. It is Johnston's belief that horses in training should be fed as many calories as they can take and his feeding routine of 16 lb of Baileys and a slice of hay had been tried and tested over eleven years.

Mark's concern was that a number of the horses were underweight and appeared not to be eating well. He had already been in touch with Baileys Horse Feeds and been assured that the composition of the concentrates preferred by his team hadn't been changed in any way. He urged senior members of staff to ensure that everyone was more aware of the importance of proper feeding, to observe closely how the horses were eating, to be more careful in measuring foodstuffs and to have a higher awareness of the horses' weights in relation to their optimum racing weights. On more than one occasion during the year I witnessed Mark scooping out feed from a horse's manger to demonstrate to staff either that the wrong amount of feed had been given or, alternatively, that a comment that the horse had not eaten up ought to have been made in the vet diary.

On May 18th Gaelic Storm came back to form in Goodwood's Forest Alliance Conditions Stakes over six furlongs under a confident and forceful ride from Kieren Fallon. On Thursday the 20th, the win statistics really ought to have been boosted further as Hammer And Sickle was kicked clear of his field approaching the distance in the EBF Ayr May Novice Stakes. However, Robbie Fitzpatrick was to learn a bitter lesson on the 7/2-on favourite, as locally-trained debutant Shatin Venture got the hang of things in the final two furlongs and crept up on his outside with a sustained run. Fitzpatrick, who clearly felt that his colt had the race in the bag, didn't have time to ask him for a further effort and failed by a neck to rectify the situation. A valuable lesson learned perhaps, but Johnston could barely conceal his anger afterwards.

A two-pronged raid on the Curragh on May 22nd saw Harryana thrown in against an Aidan O'Brien hotpot, Fasliyev, in the listed Victor Chandler Marble Hill Stakes. The filly had struck into herself when winning at Chester and probably wasn't at her best in Ireland, finishing only fifth of seven. Gaelic Storm also faced a Ballydoyle star in Bianconi, winner of the 1998 Diadem Stakes at Ascot, in the Weatherbys Ireland Greenlands Stakes, a Group 3 event over six furlongs. Sent off the 11/2 second favourite behind Bianconi, Gaelic Storm confirmed the form of his Goodwood victory, running a fine race for Kieren Fallon, responding to hard driving and failing only by a short head to repel the challenge of Kevin Ryan's Eastern Purple, ridden by Frankie Dettori. As Dettori was suspended for excessive use of the whip on the winner, Gaelic Storm can perhaps be reckoned an unlucky loser. However, his two performances boosted the yard's morale as the Tuesday morning meeting of May 25th loomed with the total number of winners for the month standing at just five.

Our conversation as we watched first lot go through their paces on the morning of May 25th was enlivened by the publication in the *Racing Post* the previous day of John Randall's and Tony Morris' selection of the top fifty trainers of the century. Mark was flattered to have been included in forty-fourth position. He also mused that he would be even more delighted to be included in such a classification of trainers for the twenty-first century, pointing out that "I have to work as hard every day to stay (at the top) as I did to get there." For Middleham's sake Mark was delighted to see that Sam Hall had made the list (at thirty-eighth), but wondered why he had been ranked so highly in comparison with such as Luca Cumani (forty-seventh). The trainer of the great Dante, Matt Peacock, was twenty-fifth, and we were intrigued by the difficulty of composing such a catalogue. With no disrespect intended to Richard Hannon, we found ourselves wondering how he could have been ranked twenty-first when John Dunlop was only thirtieth. We agreed that the classification represented a marvellous stimulus for debate and that racing folk across the country would no doubt be commenting on the rankings for some time to come. We guessed that this was probably the whole point of the exercise and, before we knew it, were back at Kingsley House ready to cross over to Warwick House for the breakfast meeting.

Johnston's attitude at the meeting was clear. Results were realistically described as terrible, the strike rate for May to date as "pretty crap". During the conversation Debbie Albion mentioned that the grass strip on the High Moor was to open that day. Johnston was dumbfounded. He had not been informed and had not taken the availability of that strip into consideration when drawing up his work lists. First lot had already exercised on the Low Moor. It was explained that fellow trainer James Bethell had telephoned the previous afternoon, spoken to one of the staff in the office, and the message had not reached Mark. Debbie thought she might have heard her staff member suggest to Mr Bethell that he call Mark directly on his mobile. In any event, Johnston was none too pleased, especially given the delay in getting access to the High Moor gallops, a delay which he reckoned had cost the yard a number of winners. The theme of feeding and the necessity of monitoring the regime and the horses' weights accurately was again raised. Johnston focused on Harryana's lacklustre run at the Curragh. He pointed out that the horse had left a scoop of feed that morning and that the weighing machine had been telling anyone who cared to consult the records that the horse was getting lighter. He drove the point home about the Efisio filly and stated that in his view at least nine horses in the yard were clearly underweight. He reiterated that the same regime was tried and tested and voiced his suspicion that the amount the horses were getting to eat had changed. It seemed to Johnston that certain groups of horses were out of condition, for example the two-year-old colts appeared well but the fillies did not. Attention to these and other details was demanded by the trainer. It was made clear that an immediate improvement would be the only acceptable outcome.

Three days later, on the 28th, signs of a recovery were at last forthcoming at Pontefract, where Kieren Fallon rode a double for the yard, firstly getting Dramatic Quest up in the Tote Conditions Stakes, despite the colt having been badly hampered early on, and then bringing Around the World, a three-year-old filly by Thatching, home in a handicap over a mile. The next day, Tissifer further encouraged hopes of a general return to form by running a much better race in the Rosehill Stakes at Doncaster, finishing three lengths behind Godolphin's promising Mutafaweq, to whom he was conceding 9 lb. It looked as though a disappointing month might just end on a high note when Hammer And Sickle gained deserved compensation under John Carroll, winning the Yarm Novice Auction Stakes at sunny Redcar.

However, events in the Bonusprint Henry II Stakes at Sandown later that afternoon were to put a damper on any positive thoughts. The Group 3 contest over an extended two miles had proved a good race for the stable in Double Trigger's heyday, and Johnston ran both Spirit of Love and the four-year-old filly Trigger Happy, the latter runner-up in the previous year's Lingfield Oaks Trial. Olivier Peslier had the mount on Spirit of Love, who disappointed badly, coming home eighth in the eleven-strong field having failed to pick up when asked shortly after the home turn. Trigger Happy fared even worse. Ridden up with the pace, she dropped tamely away to finish tailed-off last. Back to the drawing board?

A month-end tally of 8 winners at such a pivotal stage in the season was simply unacceptable to Johnston. The stable was misfiring at a time when its history suggested it ought to have been flourishing. The total of winners at the end of the month stood at 29 (Britain) and 2 (foreign). Win prize money totals had moved on to £132,237 (Britain) and £160,602 (foreign). The strike rate for May had dropped to a disappointing 7.7% (1998's May figure had been 16.7%) and the yearly percentage had declined to 12.6%. Looking for a silver lining, at least the High Moor gallops were now fully open and available. Consequently it could be reasonably expected that things would improve. Hopefully, Johnston's repeated reminders about the proper implementation of the feeding regime might also bear fruit. Above all, Fruits of Love himself was recuperating well and a run in Epsom's Coronation Cup now seemed likely. Roll on June!

CHAPTER NINE

June 1999

U nfortunately for senior staff, the first day of June coincided with yet another Tuesday morning meeting! It fell to Debbie Kettlewell to start the ball rolling by commenting on results and she pointed out that the yard was, in fact, one winner up on last year. Mark responded by saying that there had been many more runners this year, as a result of which the percentages were "pretty awful", and that in any event the achievements of 1998 provided an unambitious yardstick against which to compare this season's statistics. He went on to stress that it was crucial that the staff sought reasons for such disappointing results and asked themselves "what are we going to do about it?" Reasons might include the delay in getting access to the High Moor gallops and lack of consistency in jockey arrange-ments due to Darryll Holland's periods of suspension, but in truth he felt the problems went beyond those. More stalls preparation for the two-year-olds was prescribed and Johnston also highlighted the abysmal percentages of the older horses. He concluded that they were either not good enough, or fit enough to give of their best, or were running in the wrong races. Examples of a trademark Johnston horse, one which keeps running and running, were becoming less and less easy to find. The string in general was doing less work because there was less flesh on the horses. Mark pointed out that on most mornings exercise was being completed comfortably by 12 o'clock, whereas the year before they had struggled to finish by that time. He cited the filly Robin Lane, whose recent form had been most disappointing, as an example of a horse who required to put on weight and stressed that all senior staff should focus on those horses which could have galloped and yet had not. The message to everyone was clear: the rot had to stop and it had to be stopped by hard work and even more attention to detail.

Incidentally, Johnston takes the view that there is no such thing as 'the virus', that age-old excuse proffered by trainers when results are not going their way. To explain, obviously he agrees that viral infections can and do affect horses and their performance. Stringent precautions are taken to avoid the possibility of such infections taking root, including a comprehensive pro-gramme of vaccination. However, even though his yard has fallen victim to two influenza outbreaks over the years it has never had to stop completely and the majority of horses have always been kept working. Johnston simply does not believe in a virus which closes down yards and prevents them from having winners for months on end. He believes that stables come into and move out of form in a pattern of peaks and troughs. When the pattern is riding high and winners are flowing trainers are happy to take the credit; when the troughs are particularly low, some will say, "we've got the virus". Mark, with tongue in cheek, prefers to call this "low performance syn-drome". Sure, an actual virus might be contributing to a yard's problems, but in reality he feels that some prefer to blame a mystery illness rather than to search for other potential reasons for disappointing results—bad placing; inconclusive and unchallenging gallops; bench-mark horses running out of form, or lead horses not performing satisfactorily. His scientific training has led him to conclude that this expression is a coded message to the effect that the trainer does not have a clue as to what has gone wrong!

June also saw the arrival on these shores of leading American jockey Gary Stevens to ride for Sir Michael Stoute's powerful Newmarket yard. Johnston lost no time in snapping him up for the ride on Fruits of Love in the Vodafone Coronation Cup at Epsom on June 4th as Kieren Fallon was required to ride the favourite, Royal Anthem, for Henry Cecil's stable.

Before that excitement, however, an encouraging start was made to the month at Beverley on the evening of the 2nd when Eastways, a two-year-old colt by Efisio, ran out a winner at the third time of asking. What's more, he was followed into the winner's enclosure later that evening by the hitherto unraced three-year-old Fairy King colt Atlantic Prince, an eight-length winner of the maiden over seven and a half furlongs despite having been eased prior to the finish. Appropriately enough, the race won by Eastways was the Brian Yeardley Continental Limited 2-y-o Trophy. Mark was delighted as Brian has been one of his most loyal owners over the years.

In the period from 1993 to 1998, winners in June for Mark Johnston Racing Limited had fallen between a range of eleven to nineteen. Given May's disappointing totals it was seen as essential that June's strike rate should at least achieve the first figure. A good start to the month helped restore confidence in no small measure.

And so to Epsom for Fruits of Love's first test after the trauma of his motorway accident. The field assembled for the Coronation Cup was of the highest quality and comprised: John Dunlop's five-year-old Silver Patriarch, winner of the St Leger in 1997 and also of the Coronation Cup in 1998; Pascal Bary's Dream Well, who had completed the Prix du Jockey Club/Irish Derby double in 1998; the smart Arc-placed, ex-German mare Borgia, now trained by Andre Fabre; Henry Cecil's Royal Anthem, winner of the Canadian International at Woodbine and a horse with a massive reputation; Godolphin's Eclipse Stakes and Man o' War Stakes winner Daylami and their alleged second string Central Park, fresh from a Group 1 success in Rome's Premio Presidente della Repubblica and who had in fact finished in front of Daylami in the Dubai World Cup. A mouthwatering prospect indeed!

Although Gary Stevens had never ridden around Epsom he had enjoyed the benefit of a video masterclass from Lester Piggott as to how best to approach Epsom's roller-coaster of a track. Therefore hopes were high that the American champion, with three Kentucky Derby victories and six Breeders' Cup successes under his belt, might take over where Kieren Fallon had left off. As it turned out, the value of the race as a true test of the comparative quality of this illustrious field was lessened significantly. Central Park set no more than a muddling pace until the septet headed towards Tattenham Corner. Stevens was not alone in being deceived by this. When the tempo belatedly increased, he wasn't able to galvanise Fruits of Love into the kind of long, gradual run which the colt had produced so memorably at Nad Al Sheba, their cause probably not helped either by good to soft ground. Sensibly accepting the situation, Stevens wasn't unduly hard on Fruits of Love, the pair finishing sixth, six lengths behind Daylami, who had stalked the 2/1-favourite Royal Anthem before pouncing in the last furlong. The press chose to focus on Royal Anthem in the aftermath of the race, seeking excuses for his defeat and all but ignoring the fourth Group 1 success of Daylami in respect of whom stamina doubts had been expressed on all sides. This theme of veneration of The Thoroughbred Corporation's colt recurred throughout the season, much to both Johnston's annoyance and amusement. Though disappointed that Fruits of Love did not figure in the finish, Mark was happy that he had run well enough to confirm that he was a genuine Group 1 contender and to show that there appeared to be no lingering after-effects of his, by now, celebrated mishap. The horse had been entered for the Group 2 Hardwicke Stakes at Royal Ascot where, by all accounts, he was likely to re-oppose Royal Anthem and Mark was confident that the colt would be more competitive granted a stronger pace and a sounder surface.

In the meantime, efforts were redoubled to find some winners, and thoughts also turned to Peter Savill's Royal Rebel, who had been declared for the Prix du Jockey Club at Chantilly on Sunday June 6th. The brave run of Daliapour in finishing second to Oath in the Vodafone Derby the day before boosted connections' hopes, as Royal Rebel had been only half a length behind Daliapour at Lingfield in May. However, in testing conditions, the Chantilly race was memorable for an effortless success by Montjeu. Royal Rebel chased the pace until early in the straight before capitulating but, remembering the ground, there was no shame attached to his finishing only seventh of the eight runners.

A third success of the month was achieved the following afternoon when Mel and Jane Pilkington's Turtle turned up at odds of 11/1 in a ten-furlong seller at Pontefract. On the 9th, Mark introduced a promising two-year-old Affirmed filly named Hiddnah, whom he had bought as a yearling for $45,000 at Keeneland the previous September, in Hamilton's EBF Maiden Stakes. Johnston recalls that he had received an order from Jaber Abdullah to purchase horses at Keeneland. The owner instructed Mark to liaise with Charlie Gordon-Watson regarding proposed purchases. Johnston finds liaisons with agents impractical and awkward and, always prepared to back his own judgement, bought the filly and some other horses on his own account, thereafter circulating details of the yearlings to his owner, Jaber Abdullah included. Potential owners are invited to acquire yearlings purchased by Mark at cost and Jaber Abdullah was quick to let Johnston know that he wished to buy the Affirmed filly. By all accounts Charlie Gordon-Watson was none too pleased at the outcome of these negotiations!

Unfortunately, Sir Mark Prescott had chosen the same race to introduce a colt by Lear Fan called Sarafan, and the Hamilton crowd was treated to a well-above average contest for the course, its closing stages a match between the pair. Hiddnah, given a useful introduction by Joe Fanning, improved from mid-division to take the lead a furlong from home but, despite keeping on well up the hill, was just run out of things by Sarafan. Nonetheless, Royal Ascot plans were made for her after this promising start.

On the 12th Yavana's Pace followed up his fine run in the Yorkshire Cup by landing a listed race at Leicester over a distance just short of one and a half miles. Though the winning margin over Luca Cumani's Kadaka was only three quarters of a length, 'Yavana's' was always travelling like a winner under a confident ride from John Carroll. On the same evening card, Doonaree returned to the fray for the first time since Chester. In a match he was required to concede a stone to another Cumani-trained filly belonging to the Aga Khan, Katiykha. It was no great surprise that he struggled, especially as she developed into a decidedly useful performer later on.

Peter Savill gained some compensation for Royal Rebel's comprehensive French defeat when his 2-y-o colt Carousing, a stoutly-bred individual, who had hinted at ability in his debut race at Newcastle, justified favouritism under Kieren Fallon in a median auction stakes at Lingfield on the same evening. Given he still appeared very green, all concerned were pleased.

As Royal Ascot approached, Johnston was apprehensive, not because he lacked faith in the merit of his 'invaders' but because he realised he was "going to war without my standard bearer"—Double Trigger. Ascot had largely proved a happy hunting ground for his stable—would it do so again? The stable's only runner on the first day was Ice in the thirty-two runner Britannia Handicap. Drawn on the unfavoured side of the track, David Abell's colt finished in midfield. The stable had no runners on the second day but, even so, Johnston must have regretted that Harryana was not fit to renew rivalry with Shining Hour, as that filly swooped close home under Jimmy Fortune to land the Queen Mary Stakes. Later that afternoon, up at Hamilton, Windy Gulch, who had been running well without success, finally got her head in front in a fair six-furlong handicap. Mark had four runners on Gold Cup day. First up was Hammer And Sickle, who started fourth favourite for the Norfolk Stakes. However, he failed to shine, though he would have finished closer than eleventh but for being hampered about a furlong out. Spirit of Love duly took his place in the Gold Cup field. However, Johnston had written frankly in his *Racing Post* column the previous Saturday, pointing out that the horse had been knocking a foreleg in work, a problem which had had "a serious effect on his ability to train properly".

Nonetheless, Darryll Holland approached the race with confidence, and having tracked Cash Asmussen on John Hammond's Solo Mio, asked the colt to quicken into the lead approaching the home turn. Momentarily it looked as if Spirit of Love would pull away and emulate his illustrious former stable-companion but, almost certainly short of peak fitness, he couldn't sustain his effort, eventually finishing eighth.

After Atlantic Destiny had been outpaced in the Cork and Orrery Stakes, the spotlight fell on Hiddnah in the Chesham Stakes. Sent off at 16/1, the filly still seemed green and to be feeling the fast underfoot conditions but still managed third, three lengths behind Aidan O'Brien's Bach, staying on well at the death. Jaber Abdullah pronounced himself very pleased, and the immediate reaction from Johnston was that she should be rested, then brought back for the Fillies' Mile later in the year. At least the stable's lesser lights were keeping the flag flying, and once again the day ended with a winner when Brian Yeardley's Hormuz got the better of an odds-on favourite from Sir Michael Stoute's yard at Ripon.

As Royal Ascot's final day dawned, the stable had two runners left, Gaelic Storm, in the Wokingham Stakes, preceded by Fruits of Love, due to contest the Hardwicke Stakes some forty minutes earlier. The fates seemed to be with Johnston, as the opener at Ayr fell to his old-timer Shontaine and the Redcar curtain-raiser to an improving two-year-old Mujtahid filly called Fez, owned by the Earl of Burlington. Would Fruits of Love provide Johnston with a memorable hat trick?

Immediately after Fruits of Love's win in Dubai Johnston had nominated the Irish St Leger as his long-term target. However, after some reflection and discussion with Mick Doyle, sights were set on the King George VI and Queen Elizabeth Diamond Stakes at Ascot with a run in the Coronation Cup as his only preparatory race. He was entered in the Hardwicke Stakes but Johnston was quoted prior to Epsom as saying that the colt would only run in that if the Coronation Cup did not go to plan. The fact that plan B had had to be activated had not affected Johnston's faith in his stable star. Writing in the *Post* on June 12th he was unequivocal in his thoughts about the Ascot race: "Fruits of Love is the best. I keep telling you this, and I can assure you that you can safely disregard his form in the Coronation Cup. That race was no test."

The field for the Hardwicke, as might have been expected for a Group 2 race, was slightly less fearsome than the Coronation Cup line-up. Nonetheless, Fruity's opponents comprised: Godolphin's Sea Wave, last season's Great Voltigeur winner and trained specifically for this race; Noel Meade's Sunshine Street, who had been in the frame in the 1998 Derby and St Leger before running fifth in the Breeders' Cup Turf; Sir Michael Stoute's progressive Secret Saver; Paul Cole's battle-hardened Posidonas, winner of the John Porter Stakes and of the Hardwicke in 1998; Henry Cecil's lightly-raced Silver Rhapsody; John Dunlop's pair Sadian, fresh from victory in Chester's Ormonde Stakes, and Rabah, who had dead-heated with Nedawi in the previous year's Gordon Stakes; and of course the 6/5 favourite, Henry Cecil's Royal Anthem, the apple of the press room's eye, about whom Timeform had commented after the Coronation Cup: "after this, he's surely something of a Royal Ascot banker in the Hardwicke Stakes." As Kieren Fallon and Gary Stevens were both committed to riding for their own stables, a new jockey for Fruits of Love was required. Step forward Monsieur Peslier!

The Johnston camp was confident, especially Deirdre, Fruits of Love's regular work rider who, when giving him a spin on the track on the Friday morning was convinced he was spot on. Prior to the race preliminaries owner Mick Doyle informed Mark and Deirdre that he'd placed a substantial each-way bet. When Deirdre told him about her instincts, he promptly headed off to top up, this time on the nose.

In contrast to Epsom the early pace was strong, the gallop cut out by Johnny Murtagh on Sunshine Street, though Royal Anthem still took a keen hold with Kieren Fallon. Sea Wave was clearly ridden to shadow him, and when

Fallon drove his horse ahead with two furlongs left Frankie Dettori tried to go too. In the meantime, Olivier Peslier seemed to have read Kieren Fallon's script from Dubai. He settled Fruits of Love on the fence in rear, niggled at him to improve his position whilst still there, then pulled him out wide to challenge. Once again Fruits of Love's run proved irresistible and, passing Royal Anthem a furlong from home, he pulled clear of his field to win by an ever-increasing three lengths. Deirdre later admitted she had a tear in her eye as the colt was led into the winner's enclosure. Once again the Johnston's faith in their colt had been vindicated. True, Fruits of Love had received 2 lb from Royal Anthem, but clearly the key to victory lay not with any weight concession but with the strong pace, which had enabled Fruits of Love to give of his best and exposed Royal Anthem's slightly suspect stamina. Somewhat bizarrely, the stewards saw fit to consider the improvement in Fruits of Love's form compared to Epsom. Having received the trainer's explanation that the colt had not been suited by the slow early pace at Epsom and also appreciated the faster going at Ascot, they decided not to hold a formal inquiry.

Once again press reaction to the Hardwicke Stakes centred to an inordinate extent on Royal Anthem. In contrast to their normal attitude of "the King is dead. Long live the King!" the *Racing Post*'s front page headline on the day following the race, a busy midsummer Saturday, was "Don't Write Him Off!". No-one challenged Henry Cecil's comment that the race had come a bit too quickly for Royal Anthem after his run in the Coronation Cup. Fruits of Love had run there too, you know! Johnston added: "Everyone has been saying that this is the best Hardwicke for years and should be a Group 1 with Royal Anthem running and I hope they don't change their minds. Royal Anthem was supposed to be the best horse in Europe, so who's the best in Europe now?" I put it to Johnston that because he trains in the North as opposed to Newmarket or Lambourn his horses don't always receive the credit they deserve. Whilst he agreed this is sometimes the case, he also felt what mattered most was to win; recognition is merely icing on the cake. Asked also about what I perceived to be a bias in favour of the South in the racing press he argued that he is happy to tilt at any windmill from his Middleham stronghold and that his record had proved that there is no disadvantage being camped in the North. Nonetheless, he often wonders whether a more positive approach from his professional colleagues in the North to fight such a conception is required. "I haven't got a chip on my shoulder" states Johnston, "but sometimes I wonder if perhaps Northerners accept that they are second-best".

Amidst all the excitement at Ascot, John Carroll steered the three-year-old Sheikh Albadou filly Forum Girl to success in a seven-furlong maiden at Ayr to complete a cross-country four-timer for the stable. Over at Redcar, in addition to Fez's success, Tivoli, a three-year-old full brother to Double Eclipse and Double Trigger, showed promise in finishing second in a four-teen-furlong maiden on only his second racecourse appearance.

The upturn in the stable's fortunes continued the following week. On the 22nd Markus Graff's Mardani, a four-year-old colt by Fairy King who had raced for John Oxx in Ireland as a three-year-old, won a useful handicap at Beverley on only his third start for the Johnston yard. Two days later Aston Mara, making his debut, lifted the Newcastle United FC two-year-old maiden at Gosforth Park in good style.

On the same day a letter appeared in the *Racing Post* from Llin Golding, the Labour MP for Newcastle-under-Lyme and Treasurer of the all-party Racing and Bloodstock Committee, which contained a direct and personal attack on Peter Savill. She had revealed the line of her thinking on the matter earlier in the month when calling for closer co-operation between the BHB and the bookmakers, urging Savill to shelve the BHB's Financial Plan and to keep it on the back burner. She had further urged Savill to take note of BOLA's criticisms of the Plan. "Set it to one side", she said, "it seems to have upset a lot of people." The letter drew on these predispositions and had, as its source of inspiration, the fact that a horse owned by Savill, namely Pepperdine, trained by David Nicholls, had won the valuable William Hill

Trophy at York on 12th June, worth £38,779 to the winner. How could Savill rattle racing's begging bowl whilst helping himself to a fat bookmakers' purse, she wondered? In so far as inspiring his Saturday column was concerned this was meat and drink to Mark. "Is she seriously suggesting that Peter Savill's calls for better funding for racing would be better received if he declined any prize money his horses won? Should Socialist MPs decline their wages if they wish to call for a better deal for the poor?" Mark went on to point out that it is owners who fund the horses, staff, jockeys, box drivers, farriers, vets, etc and that those with horses entered for the William Hill Trophy had contributed £9,620 of the prize money. "It is dangerous indeed for any MP, regardless of which brand of labour—old or new—he or she favours, to propose the premise that those who have money are not allowed to speak on behalf of those who have less" reasoned Mark. His final words on the matter were "she has an obligation to learn a little more about the financial structure of the British racing industry before she stands behind the bookmakers to throw dirt at our customers."

Because of comments such as these Johnston, to coin a phrase, is often thought of as a Savillite. Whilst Peter Savill is an owner and a valued customer, Johnston supports Savill's views because he believes them to be correct and in racing's best interests, not for any blind allegiance. There is nothing Johnston likes better than a debate, especially on a subject about which he is passionate.

Winners were really starting to flow. On the 26th pocket-sized Fez was victorious at Doncaster's evening meeting under Joe Fanning in a hot little conditions stakes bringing the monthly total to fourteen. Earlier in the day, an attractive Newmarket card saw Yavana's Pace and White Heart in action for the stable. Olivier Peslier took the ride on Yavana's Pace in the Listed Fred Archer Stakes, seen by his trainer as a natural stepping stone towards another attempt at a Group race and his eventual target of the Irish St Leger. The conditions required him to concede 3 lb to Her Majesty's Blueprint and though running creditably for second, that proved too much. Even though he also tasted defeat White Heart showed himself to be in fine fettle, beaten less than 2 lengths into third by Godolphin's high-class colt Diktat in the Group 3 Van Geest Criterion Stakes.

When Mrs Belinda Strudwick's Night Shift gelding Netta Rufina responded to a first-time visor and Darryll Holland's urgings to capture a fourteen-furlong handicap at Musselburgh on June 28th he brought the final total of winners for the month to fifteen, a figure which wasn't exceptional for the stable at this time of year but which nonetheless represented a massive improvement on May's performance. I asked Mark how he accounted for the improvement? Whilst he conceded this was partly due to the "High Moor effect" he preferred to focus upon the fact that the horses were simply looking better, partly as a result of the feeding regime having been stabilised and partly because of the weather. Whatever had caused the upturn it was most welcome. Yet not everything was going to plan. At Catterick on June 30th he had two runners, Classic Lord in a two-year-old maiden race and Netta Rufina in a mile-and-a-half handicap, both ridden by Darryll Holland. Classic Lord, a two-year-old Wolfhound colt closely related to Lend A Hand, had made a satisfactory debut at Ayr and was widely expected to step up on that performance. He looked on excellent terms beforehand but, despite starting at 11/10 on, ran a dreadful race to finish fifth of twelve. An exasperated Johnston expressed frustration that he couldn't fathom out this year's two-year-olds; those he expected to win well often failing to perform at all! To make matters worse, Netta Rufina, whom he'd fancied to win in advance of a possible trip to Newmarket's July Sales, slipped on leaving the stalls, losing considerable ground. He finished powerfully but simply had too much to make up.

So, at the end of June, the total number of British winners stood at 44, with British win prize money at £276,804. The foreign statistics remained unchanged. Pleasingly, the monthly strike rate (13.3%) had improved and was also marginally better than that for June 1998 (12.9%).

CHAPTER TEN

July 1999 Part I -
The Home Front

T
wenty-four hours later, a day at Catterick brought far happier results. Mark accompanied Sheikh Maktoum's Princely Heir to Yarmouth, where the colt showed signs of a return to form for Gary Stevens in a conditions race, so Deirdre made the short trip from Middleham to Catterick. There, she saddled two three-year-olds, Stuart Morrison's Dayjur filly Tous les Jours and Sheikh Mohammed's Evesham. Both were well fancied and duly obliged, each winning by three lengths under Darryll Holland.

A flying start to the month but, then, as the overall strike rate was still disappointingly low and we were now entering a period which the evidence of the last six seasons suggested should be the most rewarding for Mark Johnston Racing Limited, it was a start the team needed. The range of winners in July during that period was fifteen to twenty-three, the highest total achieved in 1996. Typically, Johnston was acutely aware of the statistics pertaining to his business and continued to reflect upon them. Thus, at the beginning of July, he was well aware of the need to catch up with previous years if the 1999 campaign was to be as successful as everyone was hoping.

Hormuz, on the 3rd, was the first to add to the Catterick double, Joe Fanning executing a stylish piece of front running in unseasonably soft conditions at Beverley to collect an eight-and-a-half furlong handicap. On the same card, David Abell's massive two-year-old colt by Prized, Splash Out, was unfortunate to come up against Sir Mark Prescott's useful Sarafan, the 2/9 favourite, but made a race of it to finish a creditable second.

The racing highlight of Saturday July 3rd was the Coral-Eclipse Stakes at Sandown. For a variety of reasons the field could not be described as being of the very highest quality, though that's not to decry its winner, Compton Admiral, who was partnered by Darryll Holland and got home by a neck from Xaar. Held up in rear, Holland audaciously decided to stick to the inner, creeping through the field smoothly and being fortunate to find a gap at the crucial time. Unbelievably, Darryll dropped a rein a furlong from home but was able to recover and, notwithstanding the margin, his mount won a shade cleverly.

The Eclipse provided an overdue and welcome change of luck for Holland, beset by bans and controversy in recent seasons. The six-day suspension incurred at Doncaster on May 3rd for his irresponsible riding of Hammer And Sickle had taken him past the Jockey Club's fifteen-day threshold, automatically ensuring further action would be taken. Unfortunately, he'd also fallen foul of the Chester stewards on May 5th and been referred to Portman Square. Eventually, the disciplinary committee of the Jockey Club imposed a ban of fifteen days for passing that threshold, with a further sentence of six days suspended. On May 11th, Holland rode Bryan McMahon's Now Look Here in the William Hill Stakes, a handicap over seven furlongs at York. Races over this distance start on a spur which joins the round course after two furlongs or so, involving a slight turn to the left. In large fields, a high draw is often a considerable disadvantage and Now Look Here was drawn highest of all in stall 17. In an effort to overcome this Holland tacked over to his left approaching the straight. However, after leading at the distance, his mount wandered under pressure, allowing Geoff Wragg's Swallow Flight and Richard Hannon's Mayaro Bay to collar him close home. Now Look Here finished third, beaten in a finish of short heads. Unfortunately for Holland, the stewards considered his early manoeuvre to have been careless and imposed a ten-day ban. Additionally, the six days which had been suspended were now invoked. His problems didn't end there either, so his return to the limelight at Sandown came as a blessed relief to an undoubtedly talented rider.

It isn't Johnston's policy to retain a stable jockey but, over the last couple of years he's been happy to entrust the majority of rides to Darryll Holland . Mark regards Holland as an intuitive jockey. Horses run for him and he tends to make many more good decisions than poor ones. Johnston also regards Holland as being similar in style to Frankie Dettori. Interestingly, computer racing expert John Whitley, who analyses the effectiveness of jockeys riding in Britain based on how horses have run for them over a season, rated Holland second only to Ray Cochrane in 1998, a statistic which Johnston felt underpinned his opinion. Johnston does not give specific instructions to jockeys, and when he and Holland meet in the paddock they tend to swap views on their runner, remembering previous performances and any idiosyncrasies, commenting on conditions and discussing any other factors which might affect the outcome. Holland is then left to ride the race as he sees fit, not because Johnston does not have a view but rather because he recognises and respects the separate function of a jockey and does not seek to control the uncontrollable!

The stable's fortunes had almost certainly been adversely affected, particularly in May and early June, by Holland's non-availability for lengthy periods. Whilst Johnston felt it would be both improper and pointless to comment on individual decisions of the stewards without having access to all the information, both visual and verbal, available to the various panels involved, he acknowledged there is a perception in some quarters that Darryll Holland is something of a marked man. Whether true or not, it is unfortunate that the punishment meted out to him should have consequences for the stable staff in the yards affected by his suspension, such as losing out on pool money. As Mark Johnston remarked: "My yard didn't just lose a race and the prize-money that goes with it at Doncaster when Hammer And Sickle was disqualified. We also have been made to suffer for a month since. Is there any justification for that?" That said, the emergence of Joe Fanning as a more than able deputy was being viewed as something of a silver lining.

At Ripon on July 5th, Baileys Black Tie prevailed in the seller and, later on, promising displays in defeat were turned in by the handsome Hansel colt Love Blues and debutante Young Sue. The following afternoon the speedy two-year-old Kashra, full of ability but headstrong in her first three races, allowed Joe Fanning to settle her in behind in a six-furlong Pontefract nursery and, as a consequence, was able to produce a decisive turn of foot to win convincingly.

There appeared to be no stopping the yard now and July 7th brought Johnston a success that gave him almost as much pleasure as any top winner might have. At Epsom Linden Grace took the Training Grounds Median Auction Maiden, realising one of his ambitions–that of training the first winner sired by none other than his classic hero, Mister Baileys. Johnston remarked: "It was my ambition to be the first to train a winner by Mister Baileys and this was only his second runner. Linden Grace had shown plenty on the gallops but things did not look rosy three furlongs out where she went down on her nose. Darryll said she also jumped the road, so it was a smart beginning to win like she did." Incidentally, the filly is owned by Dick Moules, also one of the part owners of Double Trigger.

The following afternoon at Lingfield Island Song, a three-year-old by Saddlers' Hall who had been gelded since his previous run in May, took a fourteen-furlong handicap for Joe Fanning, justifying the 540-mile round trip from

Middleham in the process! Clearly, he would not be allowed to start at 12/1 next time. In the meantime Gaelic Storm was busy contesting the Polar Sprint Cup at Ovrevoll in Norway. Despite eight rivals, the gelding scored comfortably under Darryll Holland, relishing the soft going and setting himself up for a crack at the more valuable Polar Million Cup on July 29th.

That day, details of the acceptors for the King George VI and Queen Elizabeth Diamond Stakes were published. Fruits of Love was one of twenty-one acceptors from six countries. Early ante-post betting shows placed him as third favourite at 5/1 behind the Derby winner Oath (7/2) and Godolphin's Daylami (4/1). His old sparring partner, Royal Anthem, was a notable absentee. At the same time, a surprise announcement was made to the effect that the timetable for the Emirates World Series had been altered so that the competition would now be contained within the calendar year. To accommodate this change, instead of the King George being the first event on the schedule, the Dubai World Cup run at the end of March was deemed to have been the starting point, thus leaving Almutawakel with a handy six-point lead over his rivals.

Meanwhile, back at the yard, the daily production line of winners continued apace! On July 9th Mardani was able to dictate throughout under Darryll Holland in a rated stakes at York over a distance just short of a mile and a half. As the field looked set to swallow him up, he pulled out more to hold on by half a length. Interestingly, Darryll Holland's first words when he came back to the winner's enclosure were "November Handicap", but Johnston, sure the colt needs a sound surface, thought it unlikely the ground would be suitable at Doncaster at that stage of the season. News from Ascot came through that Allen Paulson's proposed King George challenger, the US-trained Yagli, would not now run. Updated betting forecasts showed that Fruits of Love had been supported and his odds had now shortened to 4/1.

On a downbeat note, the failure of Atlantic Destiny to run with any promise in the Listed Michael Page International Silver Trophy at Ascot on July 10th led to her being sold to race in America for Fred Seitz of Brookdale Farm. This, of course, led to Bam Bam's return to the flock and, even worse, to Johnston's worst joke of the year when, having composed a spoof lonely hearts advert for the heartbroken ewe, he stated that prospective suitors required to be "educated to Ba standard!" Deirdre is often criticised by Mark for her attempts at humour. I sincerely trust that she exacted the appropriate revenge on her husband for his!

On the same card at Ascot, the promising Dramatic Quest landed a well-contested conditions race under Darryll Holland, chiefly at the expense of John Dunlop's newcomer Meadaaar, to whom he was conceding a stone. Up at York, meantime, Tissifer was dropped to handicap company for the John Smith's Cup, a valuable contest open to three-year-olds and older horses. Only Sir Mark Prescott's Pasternak was set to carry more weight. Joe Fanning had Tissifer well placed to challenge approaching the straight but, when push came to shove, the colt was unable to pick up. Any disappointment over that performance melted away when he brought Fez home for her third successive win in the closing nursery.

Sunday July 11th saw the winning spree end. Even so, White Heart performed with credit at Hoppegarten in Germany, taking third place in the Group 2 Berlin Brandenburg Trophy over a mile.

I arrived in Middleham on July 13th to find the stable buzzing. Fruits of Love had worked on the High Moor first lot and was reckoned to be bang on target for the King George. The Johnstons were quietly confident of his prospects and Mark was generally delighted that the string was eating better, with the result that he had been able to get more fast work into them. For once, discussion of the stable's results at the weekly meeting proved to be painless!

Just one week after her Epsom debut success, Linden Grace was given a second opportunity at Doncaster's evening meeting on July 14th. However, not for the first time during the year, a fancied Johnston runner had to play second fiddle to a smart rival from Sir Mark Prescott's Heath House stables, this time in the shape of Far Mount, a winner of both his starts, at Wolverhampton and Beverley. Linden Grace seemed unsuited by the step back to six furlongs and could never quite get on terms with Far Mount.

The stable enjoyed a double on Friday July 16th courtesy of two-year-old filly Bajan Belle, who stepped up on her promising debut at Hamilton to justify favouritism at Carlisle, and Windy Gulch. The latter defied top weight in a six-furlong handicap at Hamilton's Glasgow Fair Friday evening meeting, winning well under Darryll Holland.

CHAPTER ELEVEN

July 1999 Part II -
Home Thoughts from Abroad

A
s one of the most important races of the season approached I found myself on holiday with my wife Mairi and children Michael (4) and Clare (about to become 2) in Ireland. Early on Saturday July 17th we drove from our home in Glasgow to Stranraer, caught the high-speed ferry to Belfast and then headed south. Taking advantage of a traffic snarl in Drogheda we called into a packed McDonald's for sustenance before driving further southwards, eventually arriving at our holiday accommodation in Youghal, County Cork. Before booking, my wife had checked that the accommodation offered satellite television so I would be able to keep in touch with British racing. All I needed now was to find a reliable source for my daily *Racing Post* and I would be content.

Nonetheless, I did feel disappointed, and perhaps a little guilty, that I wasn't going to be on hand during the build-up to King George day. Not that I could have done anything useful. Indeed Mark might well have been relieved that I was not going to be present at Ascot, as my visits to the racecourse were tending to coincide with disappointing runs, to such an extent that the word "jinx" was being bandied about! Any guilt was assuaged however when I read Mark's column that day, in which he described the mounting pressures, both physical and mental, associated with his stable star's new-found celebrity status. Numerous enquiries from the racing press, photographers and TV crews had been accommodated, and whilst laid-back Fruits of Love enjoyed being centre stage Mark was feeling the pressure: "It was much more fun when he wasn't so much the centre of attention. Goodness knows how heavy the burden of expectation will become next Saturday."

The same column was strangely prophetic about the chances of Johnston's Atlantic Rhapsody in the EBF Maiden at Ayr that day. Writing about the difficulties involved in choosing where to go racing when the stable had runners at five different meetings, Mark concluded he would probably go to Ayr, but for a strange reason. Noting that owner George Tiney was to travel up from Essex to see his horse run Johnston explained: "He is a horse I think a lot of but, rather than wanting to be there to see to him win, it is a case of feeling that I must be there for the post mortem if he gets beaten." Needless to say, I learned from the teletext service late that evening that Atlantic Rhapsody, sent off the 1/7 favourite, had been turned over by Linda Perratt's Howard's Lad, a 50/1 shot who had been seventh of eight at Ayr on his only previous run! Mark ought to have stayed at home with Fruits of Love. Then he might have popped down to Ripon for the finale and seen Joe Fanning make all on Young Sue for a facile success, confirming that she had made the improvement expected after her debut.

The following Tuesday Island Song followed up from Lingfield, running out an easy winner of a two-mile-one-furlong handicap at Bath. The decision to geld him now certainly seemed to have been the right one, though we never found out if Island Song agreed!

That morning's *Racing Post* had added extra spice to Saturday's King George with a story to the effect that the previous year's Prix de l'Arc de Triomphe winner, Sagamix, might well take his chance at Ascot. It had been widely expected that the colt would run elsewhere in search of softer underfoot conditions. This gave rise to the distinct possibility that Olivier Peslier would be claimed to ride Sagamix by Andre Fabre so, with Kieren Fallon committed to Oath, Johnston faced the prospect of having to find a replacement jockey for Fruits of Love. Both Gary Stevens and Michael Hills had previously ridden Fruits of Love and Johnston described them as the "obvious candidates".

Fruits of Love, now as low as 3/1 with Ladbrokes, was going to be well supported at Ascot, not only by punters but also by the four vets and nine Hertfordshire firemen involved in his rescue earlier in the year. What's more, owner Mick Doyle issued an invitation to them all to join him in his box commenting: "It is the least I could do because had they not acted so bravely and done their jobs as professionally as they did Fruits of Love would not be at Ascot and possibly may not even be alive. This is my way of saying thank you to them."

As press speculation about the possibility of a slow gallop in the big race mounted Johnston was asked whether Fruits of Love might go on if the pace was slow. He replied: "What happened at Epsom was beyond a joke and we don't want a repeat. I don't want to rule out making it if there's no gallop, but all the jockeys will be very aware of what happened at Epsom."

Meantime, at Leicester on July 21st, Robin Lane continued her return to form with a creditable second place. Otherwise stable runners were few and far between as Fruits of Love's moment of truth loomed. However, the *Racing Post Weekender* published on July 21st made me seethe the whole day long. I found myself reading the paper on Youghal's delightful Claycastle Beach during some uncharacteristically hot County Cork weather. To explain, after the Hardwicke Stakes Johnston had taken delight in knocking the press corps' habit of hyping the status of a race only to decry it if the result failed to conform to their predictions. Many of the press had touted Royal Anthem as the best horse in Europe prior to that race and after Fruits of Love's comprehensive victory Johnston had mockingly asked "Who's the best horse in Europe now?" *The Weekender* returned fire.

Chris McGrath took up the attack: "How, to begin with, can anyone back Fruits of Love or Silver Patriarch? At this trip they both need to be produced from off a sound gallop …. Both Fruits of Love and Silver Patriarch were embarrassed trying to quicken off a slow pace there (at Epsom) and connections of the grey horse are sufficiently anxious to be considering making the running. Even those of Fruits of Love, the best horse of all time, may become prey to an element of self doubt." Colleague Malcolm Heyhoe took up the baton thus: "I can't see any point though taking the 4/1 about Fruits of Love. This is a bad price for a horse who couldn't live with Daylami in the Coronation Cup and who was probably flattered by his Hardwicke win from a below-par Royal Anthem and an overrated Sea Wave." How I hoped 'Fruity' would make them eat their words on Saturday!

On the same day in the *Post*, Mark had criticised the Ascot executive's decision to water in advance of the King George. Seven millimetres of water had been put on the track on Monday July 19th and a further two millimetres of rain fell that night. Johnston was concerned that extensive watering would favour such as Oath, Daliapour and possibly even Daylami (all from top Newmarket stables) whilst inconveniencing Fruits of Love. Johnston said: "Fruits of Love wants fast ground. The King George is a high summer race and ought to be run on fastish going. I don't understand why they are watering with rain forecast on Wednesday and Thursday." Ascot's Clerk of the Course, Nick Cheyne, was quoted in the *Racing Post,* faintly ridiculously, as saying: "We are not watering to change the ground. We are watering to make sure the ground is no worse than good to firm." Cheyne had already found himself under pressure regarding the ground from other trainers. Henry Cecil was quoted on the previous Sunday as saying he would rather have good ground for Oath, a wish shared by Luca Cumani for Daliapour. Johnston's incursion into the debate was designed to ensure that Ascot thought twice before further extensive watering and was a move calculated to maximise any potential advantage to his own runner. It reminded me of Sir Alex Ferguson's wily tactic before his Manchester United side clashed with Inter Milan at the San Siro stadium in the Champions' League earlier in the year. By highlighting what he perceived as a potential problem in getting a strong enough referee he did his best to ensure that the officials appointed by UEFA would be very aware they were under close scrutiny, thus lessening the chance of controversial decisions going against his side.

The good news on July 21st was that Olivier Peslier would definitely be free to ride Fruits of Love, Andre Fabre having revealed that after a disappointing scope, Sagamix would wait for an autumn campaign.

As the race crept closer, positive noises were coming from Oath's camp. Willie Carson, racing manager to the owners, The Thoroughbred Corporation, was very bullish and all the major bookmakers made Oath favourite ahead of Daylami and Fruits of Love. Godolphin also announced that Nedawi would run in the big race. Since chasing home Fruits of Love in Dubai, the St Leger winner had finished fifth in the Ascot Gold Cup, not quite lasting two and a half miles. Suspicions were aroused that he might have been entered to act as a pacemaker for Daylami, but his inclusion in the field seemed positive from Johnston's point of view as not only would he be likely to ensure a good pace but history had shown that Fruits of Love had the beating of him.

Friday's paper brought the final declarations. 'Fruity' would face the Derby first and second, Oath and Daliapour, multiple Group 1 winner Daylami and his stable-mate Nedawi, John Dunlop's Silver Patriarch, Noel Meade's Sunshine Street, who had been fourth in the Hardwicke and the Hong Kong raider, Ivan Allan's Indigenous, the mount of Cash Asmussen, who had beaten Fruits of Love in the Hong Kong International in December 1998. Fruits of Love remained third favourite but betting confidence behind Oath was growing.

Back in Youghal, keeping tabs on British racing was proving a little more difficult than I had anticipated. True, our apartment did boast satellite television, but unfortunately the pre-set channels did not include any offering racing and the BBC was not available. Calls were made home to have the race taped and the local press was scoured for any sign that the King George might be broadcast on RTE. The realisation dawned that I would have to watch the race from one of the local bookmakers' offices, no great hardship in itself but a task complicated by the need to make arrangements for the children to be kept happy when they would much rather be at the beach or off swimming etc! The glorious weather had continued all week.

My first aim on King George Day itself, Saturday July 24th, was to get hold of a *Racing Post*. How would its pundits see things developing? How would Fruits of Love's chances be assessed? Irritatingly, the answers remained unknown to me for a half hour or so after purchase of the paper. My four-year-old son, Michael, who had accompanied me on my walk from the Carleton Wharf apartments to Read and Write in North Main Street, just beyond Youghal's landmark Clock Tower, insisted that I buy him an ice cream as a price for the pleasure of his company. The return saw me perform feats of astounding dexterity in an effort to prevent excess ice cream dripping onto my pristine paper, whilst at the same time keeping an eye on Michael's traffic awareness. Coincidentally, Michael's date of birth was just four days after Fruits of Love's foaling, but we have yet to establish any going preferences for him, far less enter him in a Group 1 toddlers' race!

Back at base I scanned the paper excitedly. Henry Cecil and Kieren Fallon were both confident about the Derby winner's chances. It was reported that Frankie Dettori had been equally effusive in his praise of Daylami in a BBC Television interview on Friday. In his regular Saturday column, Mark wrote of the difficulties inherent in coping with the pressures of training a top racehorse: "It is hard to describe what it feels like to have such a precious animal under one's care, to have to take him out and exercise him every day, to have to put him under physical pressure to keep him fit and to worry about him returning in one piece. I have been counting every hour in the run-up to this race. So far, so good, and he's in great shape. He is as near spot on as we can possibly get him. All we need now is a good pace on fast ground." He also explained his position over the watering controversy: "It was probably a bit harsh to say that I 'attacked' or 'blasted' Ascot for their watering policy this week. I simply questioned the fact that they were watering in the face of a weather forecast which predicted showers, some heavy. I hope that they haven't had any and that the ground will still be on the fast side, as the course predicted. But I did feel that they were playing with the chances of a number of the runners, including mine. I reiterate that I will be most upset if the ground ends up softer than good, patchy, or slower than you'd expect in July." Once again he touched upon one of his favourite hobby horses, namely early-closing races, highlighting his view that the only reason races closed in this way was to bolster the prize with owners' money in effect "just to be in". The motivation for his comments was the wellbeing of his owners, "I am not looking for my owners to be subsidised by anyone, as is continually asserted by various sections of the media, but I am sick of them being ripped off." Melvyn Collier's influential Pricewise column sided with Daylami, dismissing Fruits of Love as 'over-hyped', which seemed a bit rich, to say the least!

The *Racing Post* also featured an article by Tony O'Hehir on Mick Doyle, Fruits of Love's owner. A native of Redcross, County Wicklow, Mick now lives in Killybegs, County Donegal, from where he operates his supertrawler and fish processing business. The first horse which Mick had owned outright was Johnston's Loveyoumillions, winner of the Tattersalls Breeders' Stakes at the Curragh. There had been several decent animals since and Mick fondly recalled dealings with Godolphin over his star two-year-old Mick's Love: "There have been a few other decent horses like Mick's Love—Godolphin bought him off me; I hope they haven't forgotten my number—but Fruits of Love has surpassed everything else."

Paul Haigh entitled his piece the "Column for Losers" and proceeded to try to find the winner of the race by identifying those runners who couldn't win. A cunning plan, but one which came unstuck when he had ruled out the entire field on this basis! Fruits of Love's dismissal was on the following grounds: "Fruits of Love can't win because he likes firm ground which he isn't quite going to get either because there has been watering. Anyway, in the Hardwicke he 'only' beat Royal Anthem who, however hard interested parties may try to talk him up, is definitely no world beater at a mile and a half. Also, King George winners are not trained in Yorkshire. This latter piece of information is sad, but true."

My eye was also caught by a tiny item on page 10 of the *Post* which pointed out that although the King George had retained sufficient prestige to have been included in the nine-race roster for the Emirates World Series, the prize money on offer made it only the forty-first most valuable race in the world in 1998. Bearing that statistic in mind made me wonder at those who had viewed Sheikh Mohammed's veiled threat to withdraw from British racing in his speech at the Gimcrack Dinner on December 9th 1997 as less than serious. Did they really imagine that such a race would have been included in the World Series schedule had it not been for the continuing patronage of British racing by the Maktoums?

I also noticed a piece about Henry Cecil's views on how the favourite Oath might fare in the pre-race parade. The colt had become upset at Epsom where Kieren Fallon had broken early from it, incurring a fine in the process. Cecil commented: "I don't know how he will take it. I would rather there wasn't a parade but I'm not going to get upset about it. If Oath goes berserk, I am not having him hurt himself. It wouldn't be fair on the people who backed him, but we will take things as they come." It seemed to me that the measure of a great racehorse must include a good racing temperament in addition to the ability to run well; as for the 'backers', had not Cecil taken into account that many a punter might have passed over Oath because of his agitated performance in the Derby parade?

To settle my nerves before the big race (God only knows how the Johnstons and Mick Doyle must have been feeling), Mairi and I decided to take the children to lunch at Moll Goggin's Bar and Bistro at Carleton Wharf. Dining al fresco in the warm sunshine and enjoying a glass or two of something to calm me down, I reflected on the press coverage, at the same time hoping against hope that Fruits of Love would show his true colours and prove, amongst other things, that being trained in Yorkshire was no barrier to success at the very highest level. Having become suitably mellow my eye was drawn to 'the legend of Moll Goggin' printed on the menus and also on transfers on the windows of the bar. Let me recount the sorry tale.

Moll Goggin was the only daughter of a wealthy Youghal shopkeeper. She was a beautiful young woman and many local men sought her hand in marriage. Much to the distress of her parents she fell in love with a local sailor. But Moll's happiness was to be short-lived. Soon the sailor's ship was ready to sail and he and Moll were forced apart.

On the eve of his departure, Moll and her lover walked to the point just beyond the lighthouse which now bears her name. As the sun set over the bay, Moll embraced and kissed her lover tenderly. She vowed that she would await his return and would always remain faithful to him. The sailor promised that when his ship returned to port they would meet at the same place and be together forever.

The following morning his ship set sail and Moll waved farewell as it disappeared over the horizon. A few days later the ship encountered a violent storm; all hands were lost and the ship was never seen again. Unaware of its fate, Moll continued her lonely vigil on the clifftop awaiting her lover's return. As the months passed by with no news of the ship or its crew Moll became increasingly distraught, and her anguish turned to distraction. Finally, in the dim light of an October evening, Moll saw the spirit of her lover approaching. Overjoyed, she rushed into his ghostly embrace only to perish on the rocks below!

Little did I know that the events of the afternoon would cause me to reflect upon this legend quite so soon!

We made our way from Carleton Wharf into the town on foot. Youghal is famous as the location used for the filming of the classic "Moby Dick". Whilst I sought Cashman's bookmakers in North Main Street, Mairi and the children lingered around the small square which leads from the main street to the harbour.

At post time, Oath was 9/4 favourite, with Daylami on offer at 3/1 and Fruits of Love at 4/1. A small crowd had gathered in Cashman's to watch the race, but I was struck by how quiet they were as it unfolded. My single yell of "Go on, Peslier!" seemed to reverberate around the room—perhaps my strident Scottish accent didn't sit well with the soft County Cork brogue! The race seemed to be over in a flash. True, Fruits of Love did not have a clear run at a crucial time but the winner, Daylami, had flown clear before Peslier got him going from a position well in rear. In the circumstances, Fruits of Love did well to take third place, half a length behind his old rival Nedawi, the pair five lengths adrift of the impressive Daylami. The younger generation, represented by the Derby pairing of Oath and Daliapour, finished second-last and last of the eight runners.

As I saw things Peslier had set Fruits of Love an impossible task. The key to his successes in Dubai and at Ascot had been a long, gradual run. Here, Peslier seemed to want to be in rear for the sake of it and waited so long there that in my household he will forever be known as Moll Goggin! By the time he produced Fruits of Love, having taken the wrong option in passing Indigenous, Daylami had gone for home and, whilst it is difficult to take anything away from such a clear winner, I had no doubts that Fruits of Love would have given Daylami much more of a race had Peslier asked him for his effort at the time I was urging him to do so in Cashman's. At the very least he would have finished second, and the difference between that and third place was £66,000 and, even more importantly, two points in the World Series rankings.

Deflated and disappointed, I made my way back to join the family. As we headed for the beach to allow Michael and Clare to play in the late afternoon sun, we passed Moll Goggin's corner and I told Mairi about how I had seen Olivier Peslier in that role during the race. To take my mind off things, Michael and I set ourselves to digging channels for the incoming tide to invade. I couldn't help but wonder, though, how Mark was feeling in the aftermath.

Sunday's *Racing Post* was rightly effusive in its praise of Daylami. Alastair Down pointed out that the horse had now won five Group 1s in four different countries, at distances from a mile to a mile and a half and on terrain varying from very soft to firm. Yet he was still to receive the credit he deserved: "He has never really captured the heart", said Down, "but those who were not taken with this performance must have tickers of stone or simply never give credit where it is palpably due." What of Fruits of Love? Moll Goggin (sorry, Olivier Peslier) indicated that he was less than impressed by the antics of Cash Asmussen on Indigenous, who he claimed "all the way was going left and right like a snake". This, he said had hindered his chance of being better placed going into the straight. The *Post* also carried a view from Mark Johnston who started by saying how nervous he'd been: "Thank God it's over! It was just like the Double Trigger days. I was so nervous I can't describe it. Every step Fruits of Love took in the few days leading to the King George I was terrified he was going to slip up or do something awful." Such is Johnston's intensity, such are the inner demons which drive him on towards higher and higher goals, that I can well imagine how on edge he would have been. Of the race itself, Mark commented: "Hand on heart I have to say I'm disappointed with third place. Fruits of Love was better than he's ever been and I truly thought he could win. He's put up a great effort, but I was never as happy with him as I was in the Hardwicke. Half a mile out he was travelling far too easily at the back of the field. They sprinted off the home bend and he was never going to peg them back. The way the race was run gave my fellow a huge amount to do. I don't want to be accused of sour grapes—the winner won so well—but if any horse had some sort of an excuse it was Fruits of Love. A lot of things went wrong. Olivier said Indigenous kept swinging from side to side in front of him putting him in a quandary as to which way to go. They got squeezed a bit and were lucky to get through. At least his final placing banishes any talk of his being inconsistent and we can still think in terms of challenging for other World Series races, such as the Canadian International, the Breeders' Cup Turf and the Japan Cup."

One bizarre footnote to the race was the stewards' reaction to Oath's breaking early from the parade. Kieren Fallon was fined £1,250 for breaching the rules. Mark later commented: "I am a big fan of Henry Cecil and Kieren Fallon, but I was disappointed to see them skip part of the pre-race parade with Oath. Most of us regard parades as a necessary evil, something we could do without but are forced to take part in. So what will it take to stop Henry and Kieren from breaking the rules as they did here and at Epsom?" The Ascot stewards in their wisdom fined only Fallon. Henry Cecil was not at the enquiry but was represented. Stewards' secretary Ashley Bealby said Fallon had been fined, but not Cecil, as it was felt that the jockey was "in charge" of Oath at that point. The stewards decided that Oath had been allowed to leave the parade early "without sufficient reason". Can we presume, then, that neither the stewards nor their secretary had read Cecil's comments in the previous day's *Post*? Or should we draw our own conclusions as to why Cecil should have escaped punishment? Would a Yorkshire trainer who had signalled his intentions in such a manner have been dealt with similarly? In my view he would not.

Onward from Ascot then, disappointed but with faith in the stable's star unshaken. As if to compensate for their illustrious stable-companion's defeat, Hiddnah, St Helensfield and Star Rage all put their best foot forward to win on King George day, the first two obliging at Newcastle and the last-named at Redcar. Alan Lillingston's filly Rafting resumed winning ways at Chester's Sunday meeting on July 25th and, the following day, the rejuvenated Island Song completed a hat-trick when winning again at Folkestone.

The string clearly remained in good form and Johnston was buoyant as Goodwood beckoned. The Sussex meeting is one of his highlights of the racing year. A strong team had been assembled and now that the horses were in such fine fettle, good results were anticipated. On the first day, Kashra again settled nicely for Darryll Holland before pouncing to win the Evening Standard Nursery Stakes. On dismounting, Holland told Mark that despite her current lenient handicap he thought she could be up to Group class. Up at Beverley on the same day, the stoutly-bred two-year-old colt High Cheviot (by Shirley Heights, out of a winner over an extended ten furlongs) began his career pleasingly. Despite seeming very green he still got to within a short head of Tim Easterby's Lady Helen over a trip of just seven and a half furlongs; an encouraging start indeed.

On the second day of Goodwood, Wednesday July 28th, the stable's only runner was the two-year-old Break the Code, who showed improved form under Michael Roberts to finish second in the thirteen-runner Selsey Maiden Stakes. On the third, Thekryaati finally produced something like his all-weather form on turf, landing a valuable twenty-two runner handicap under Olivier Peslier at odds of 16/1. Friday's meeting was frustrating, Mardani, Fez and Acicula all failing narrowly to hit the target, finishing second, whilst Royal Rebel's first run since the French Derby was disappointing. Under 9 st 7 lb in a hot handicap he was, perhaps, ridden a little close to the pace and unable to pick up when driven, eventually finishing tenth to Henry Cecil's Azouz Pasha.

Mark's Goodwood raiding party was completed by Peter Savill's Carousing in the Vodafone Nursery Stakes on Saturday July 31st. The least experienced runner in a thirteen-strong field, he justified favouritism under Kieren Fallon, staying on willingly. The Goodwood meeting had coincided with the dramatic sacking of Fallon as stable jockey by Henry Cecil for reasons best and sufficiently described as "personal". That Fallon is as talented a jockey as there is riding in Europe is undeniable; however, given what Tom O'Ryan, writing in the *Racing Post*, described as "his uncanny knack of courting controversy" it was hard to argue with his description of the jockey as a "flawed genius".

The Polar Million Cup, in which Gaelic Storm faced eleven rivals, was run at Ovrevoll on July 29th. His biggest danger was reckoned to be Pistachio, the only three-year-old in the race and formerly trained at Newmarket by James Fanshawe, for whom he'd failed narrowly to win the Two Year Old Trophy at Redcar. The local raider ran well, but Gaelic Storm was always holding any challenge and duly won by a length, earning a first prize of £40,290 in the process.

As the month ended, Johnston sent a posse of five runners to Thirsk. Amarice and a well-bred debutante called Singing Winds both gained a place. The other three, Happy Diamond, Lady Melbourne and Rafting all started favourite and won, providing a treble for Darryll Holland. Saturday July 31st also coincided with our return from holiday to Glasgow. Happily, a brief wait in the Belfast terminal of the Stena Line coincided with Rafting's televised win. Talking of televisions, I had discovered much to my chagrin and to Mairi's amusement that the Racing Channel had been available at Carleton Wharf after all. The sweltering weather had meant that our visits to Moll Goggin's had been confined to sitting outside in the sun with our drinks. To my horror, I realised on the penultimate day that there was a screen permanently tuned to the Racing Channel on the inner face of the front wall of the bar!

That late flurry of activity brought the total number of winners for the month of July to 27, setting a new record for any month in the history of Mark Johnston Racing Limited. Johnston pronounced himself pleased with the effort, although in keeping with his ethos of self criticism expressed his pleasure by saying that the statistic "took the pressure off" for a while. Win prize money totals had moved on to £402,133 (British) and £210,924 (foreign) and the excellent monthly strike rate of 25.5% moved the seasonal rate to 15.6%. The cumulative total of British winners for the year now stood at 69.

Deirdre & Mark Johnston

Middleham—steeped in history and horseracing

Second lot heading for the gallops

Kingsley House

On Low Moor

Quick Ransom and Dean McKeown join connections in the winner's enclosure after the 1992 Ebor at York

September '95; Branston Abby, a stalwart of the yard from 1992 until 1996, records victory number nineteen in the Sceptre Stakes at Doncaster

Mister Baileys bringing classic glory back to Middleham; he holds on from Grand Lodge in the 1994 2000 Guineas

The Johnston-trained brothers Double Trigger (blaze) & Double Eclipse fight out the finish of the 1995 Goodwood Cup

September '98; Double Trigger becomes the first horse since Beeswing in 1841 to win the Doncaster Cup for a third time

Double Trigger returns after his historic 1998 Doncaster Cup victory. (Inset) Double Trigger had a train named after him in 1999

Bijou d' Inde (left) thwarts Ashkalani in the 1996 St James's Palace Stakes at Royal Ascot

The Team

Debbie Albion

Robynne Watton

Jock Bennett

Bobby Elliott

Joe Fanning

Mark on a cold morning

Mark with Sheikh Maktoum al Maktoum (centre)

Johnston's first winner outside Europe—and the second-biggest prize of his career: Fruits of Love (near side) wins the Dubai Turf Classic

*April; Rafting (with Gail Alderson) after becoming
Johnston's ninth winner of the month*

*18th June, 1999—a red-letter day for Kingsley House.
Shontaine's win at Ayr is the first leg of a cross-country four-timer ...*

... an hour later; Fruits of Love routs a top-class field in the Hardwicke Stakes at Royal Ascot

Fruits of Love is led in after his Royal Ascot victory

Dr Sarah Freeman pictured with the Duke of Richmond after receiving the Lanson Racing Lady of the Year award. It was Sarah who risked her life to save Fruits of Love after the M25 accident

Netta Rufina brings the stable's June total to fifteen—a massive improvement on May's performance—as he captures a handicap at Musselburgh

Yavana's Pace wins the listed March Stakes at Goodwood at the end of August

*Cool Investment makes a winning debut under Joe Fanning
at Musselburgh in September*

*September—a valuable nursery at Hamilton and Maktoum al Maktoum's Golden
Miracle finally gets his head in front, beating stable-companion Glenwhargen*

*Kayo and Joe Fanning at Newcastle after recording Johnston's
one-hundredth winner of 1999*

One for the future? Yavana's Pace's full sister Littlepacepaddocks obliges on her racecourse debut at Musselburgh in November...

...the second of Virgin Soldier's six successive autumn wins comes on the same day

CHAPTER TWELVE

August 1999

opes were high at Klampenborg in Denmark on August 1st for Yavana's Pace's chances in the Scandinavian Open Championship over a mile and a half. However, the prevailing ground conditions of "very firm" were really against the gelding and he failed by a short head to hold the Norwegian-trained Albaran, who had also won the race the year before. The long-term goal for Yavana's Pace remained the Irish St Leger and with that in mind Mark began searching for a suitable warm up.

The stable got off the mark at Carlisle's evening meeting on the 2nd, Love Blues just lasting home in a twelve-furlong handicap. Thereafter Windy Gulch followed up by landing the odds at Newcastle two days later. Once again a solid start had been made to the month. Johnston looked forward to Gaelic Storm's next Scandinavian adventure on August 8th, this time at Jagersro in Sweden. Gaelic Storm had collected just under £60,000 for his two wins in Norway and was now set to compete for about £11,000 in the Zawawi Baltic Cup on dirt. Regular pilot Darryll Holland had flown to Sweden with Mark but, incredibly, failed to appear on time for the race. Therefore Johnston had to engage the services of Scandinavian champion Kim Andersen at short notice. Gaelic Storm isn't the most straightforward of rides and there's little doubt that Holland's presence would have led to a better performance. As it was, he finished third, three lengths behind the winner State of Caution, who had been claimed by Mr Claes Bjorling after winning over seven-furlongs at Wolverhampton for Karl Burke in February. In fairness to Andersen, Gaelic Storm patently did not enjoy the surface. When Holland finally appeared, after Mark had left the course, he sensationally failed an alcohol test and was prevented from taking his ride in the Swedish Derby. By all accounts, when Johnston had left to visit the stables in the morning Holland had stayed behind, apparently under the impression that Gaelic Storm's race was not until mid-afternoon. "I went out for a spot of lunch and had one glass of wine" explained Holland. "I was amazed when I got to the course forty-five minutes before what I thought was the time of Gaelic Storm's race to find it had already been run. I must have got it confused with the time of the Derby—and as if that wasn't bad enough I then failed the alcohol test." The local stewards also refused to allow him to take his remaining rides. Furthermore, he was fined 3,000 Swedish kroner (about £230).

Holland's behaviour sparked off considerable press speculation as to whether Johnston would continue to utilise his services. Mark described the incident as "an unprofessional act which let down the whole team" adding he was "fed up and disappointed by the incident." In fact Johnston was more concerned by Holland's failure to appear than by the drink offence, the Swedish alcohol threshold being considerably lower than the British equivalent. For a short while after that Holland was not offered many rides, but gradually their relationship got back on tracks, partly because Mark hoped the incident might have taught Holland a lesson and also because he feels that jockeys generally are not paragons of reliability. In short, he felt it would have been unfair to have gone completely overboard about Holland's behaviour.

David Abell's Splash Out duly won his maiden at Ayr on August 10th, the veteran Star Rage lifted a Beverley handicap over an extended two miles on the following afternoon and the consistent but unlucky filly Caerosa enjoyed success at Hamilton on the evening of the 11th. However, though a tally of five winners after a third of the month had passed was good, plenty more were required to match 1995 and 1997, when twenty-two had been achieved in the month.

Mick Doyle's Love Lane did his bit to keep the numbers ticking over when successful in a Beverley nursery under top weight on the 12th, and it came as no surprise when Lord Hartington's Awake (1/3 favourite), a two-year-old colt by First Trump, confirmed he'd clearly benefited from a promising Leicester debut to win Epsom's Staff Ingham Maiden Stakes the following evening. Kieren Fallon had been booked to ride him but failed to appear on time. As this was the first race on an evening card, replacement jockeys were few and far between. Johnston approached Michael Tebbutt to take the ride and he was happy to do so. However, shortly after agreeing this, Michael Roberts walked into the weighing room (his first scheduled ride was in the fifth race). Mark teased Michael that if he had arrived five minutes earlier the ride would have been his. Michael Tebbutt, who overheard the remark, approached Mark to say that if he preferred Michael Roberts he would willingly stand down. Johnston indicated he would prefer Roberts, simply because he had ridden regularly for his stable before, and the switch was duly made. Johnston was greatly impressed by Tebbutt's gesture and resolved to repay the favour some day. Forty minutes later, Robin Lane made it an evening double for the stable in a Classified Stakes at Warwick, making all to gain her first success of the year.

On August 14th the *Racing Post* reported that a unique honour was to be conferred upon Double Trigger. Great North Eastern Railways, the sponsors of the Doncaster Cup, had decided to name one of their engines after him. GNER's Press and PR Manager, David Mallender, pointed out that this was the first time since the demise of the age of steam that an engine had been named after a racehorse. One of Double Trigger's owners, Ron Huggins, was delighted by the move, revealing that Doncaster's Racecourse Executive had commissioned a sculpture of the great horse. The story concluded by stating that a special naming ceremony for the engine would take place at London's

Kings Cross station on September 8th, the day before the Doncaster Cup. Mark couldn't resist writing about the news in his column that day, in the process revealing an in-depth knowledge of Thomas the Tank Engine stories. Doubtless this knowledge was gleaned from Charlie and Angus, but suddenly a horrible realisation dawned—I had never seen Mark Johnston and the Fat Controller together!

At Windsor on August 16th, Mark fielded an interesting runner in Happy Change, owned by The Winning Line. Happy Change had shown smart form on the flat in Germany before joining Venetia Williams with a view to a tilt at the Champion Hurdle. He'd last run on the flat for her eleven months ago. Having endured training problems he was sent to Johnston chiefly because of the swimming pool at Kingsley House. The race chosen for his comeback was a conditions event over a mile and a quarter and he ran well enough to finish second behind Jeremy Noseda's Goombayland. Not unnaturally after such a long lay off, he left the impression the outing would do him good.

York's Ebor meeting began on August 17th and Mark was hopeful of a good show on what he regards as home territory. Unfortunately, Linden Grace ran too badly to be true in the Acomb Stakes, a race previously won for the stable by Bijou d'Inde. The stable wasn't represented in the Juddmonte International Stakes, won by Royal Anthem in a style that went some way to justifying the superlatives previously heaped on him. Johnston's Windy Gulch performed well enough in the six-furlong handicap, leading at the distance before being swallowed up by those drawn high but, in the midst of a heavy shower which changed the ground from good to firm to good, Splash Out ran no sort of a race in the concluding Eglinton Nursery Handicap.

Having stayed in Middleham on the evening prior to the start of York I drove home after racing so that I could witness my son Michael's first day at primary school. The programme which the school had lined up for us did not finish until 11 am, after which I made a mad dash south in an effort to reach York in time to see Yavana's Pace and Mardani run in the Tote Ebor. Just as the

Yorkshire Oaks was taking place (2.35), indeed as Ramruma was crossing the line in first place, I was discreetly changing clothes inside my parked car! I finally made it onto the course in time to see Darryll Holland part company with top weight Yavana's Pace en route to the start, a manoeuvre which led to Mark getting some unscheduled exercise, being forced to lead the horse part of the way. In the event, neither Yavana's Pace nor Mardani shone. Johnston has a theory that in order to win the Ebor a horse has to run close to the pace, as the leaders tend to form an arrowhead, thereby making it difficult to come out of (or go round) the pack without giving away too much ground. Yavana's Pace endured a rough passage, jostled about in the pack and going from mid division to a position in rear at just the wrong time. Eventually switched wide, he immediately endured a jostling match with Theatreworld for much of the straight before Holland finally accepted defeat. On the other hand Mardani, ridden by Gary Stevens, held the perfect position until turning for home at which point he began treading water. Perhaps he didn't stay, though a more plausible excuse was that the rain-softened going had gone against him.

The final day of the York meeting coincided with a visit to the yard in the morning by Joe Mercer and Bruce Raymond, who came to discuss the horses they manage on behalf of the Gainsborough operation. Given the numbers involved, I was greatly impressed by the slick way in which the staff prepared then pulled out each one in turn, allowing Joe and Bruce to examine them, at the same time discussing their past performances and future prospects with Mark. After the tour of inspection, I travelled to the races with Mark, where the stable had two horses engaged, Let It Rain and Gaelic Storm. Let It Rain was running in the Bradford and Bingley Rated Stakes over a distance just short of a mile and, in letting him take his chance, Mark broke one of his golden rules—the horse was 1 lb out of the handicap! In fact, he ran very well, belying odds of 33/1. Twenty runners led to an incident-packed race. At the time Mark commented on interference caused to Let It Rain on the home turn, but for which he felt the horse might have won. His reaction immediately afterwards (Let It Rain had finished fifth, though at the time we mistakenly thought fourth) was that the horse was unlucky. So, when we heard a stewards' inquiry called, we made our way to the weighing room thinking Jason Tate on Refuse to Lose might be adjudged the guilty party and hoping that Let It Rain might be promoted to third. To Mark's amazement, when we got there we found Darryll Holland and Tony Culhane (Night of Glass' jockey) standing outside the stewards' room and, surprise surprise, the eventual outcome was that Darryll was suspended for three days for irresponsible riding in the final furlong, the stewards having taken the view that his mount had caused minor interference to Night of Glass. Mark approached the stewards' secretary to enquire whether the stewards had considered the incident in which his horse had sustained interference on the bend. He was invited to view the race in the stewards' room and, a little while later, emerged blazing mad.

The stewards did not share his view of the incident. Indeed they advised Johnston that in their opinion any trouble met by Let It Rain on the bend resulted from Darryll Holland's failure to keep proper control of the horse rather than any other cause. Incredulous at this outcome, we made our way to the Ebor restaurant where one of Mark's owners, Mel Pilkington, and his wife Jane, were entertaining senior members of their staff. The result of the stewards' inquiry was being made known as we shared the lift with Mel; he was amazed at their findings too!

Unsurprisingly, Johnston wrote about this apparent injustice at length in his Saturday column on August 21st. He pointed out that the stewards' interpretation of the incident on the bend was not shared by the *Racing Post*'s race reader who had written that Let it Rain "lost ground when meeting interference turning for home. In the circumstances he did very well to finish as close as he did." Mark added his exasperation by concluding: "The Jockey Club assures us that there is no victimisation of particular jockeys, but is it any wonder we are not always convinced?"

In the final race of the meeting, the City of York Stakes, Gaelic Storm was unlucky to come up against Godolphin's smart Fa-Eq, receiving 5 lb, and in the circumstances was not disgraced in fourth. Gaelic Storm's ideal distance requirements are problematical in that, in a perfect world, he needs a trip of six and a half furlongs, tending to be outpaced over an easy six and often finding seven furlongs stretching his stamina just too far. Johnston had quipped in his column on the preceding Saturday that "there is no truth whatsoever in the rumour that I only chose this race for him because it is due to be run at 5.30 and all the jockeys should have arrived by then." In the paddock before the race he also relayed to owner, Ian Harland, the terms of an e-mail I had sent to Mark after reading the news that GNER was to name an engine after Trigger. I had suggested that GNER should use Mark and Darryll Holland in an advertising campaign, perhaps picturing them stepping onto the new engine together above a caption which would read "We'll get you there on time!" I'm glad to say that the joke was taken in good part by all concerned. Thus a disappointing, if eventful, York drew to a close. Fortunately, spirits were raised immediately the next day when David Abell's Paradise Garden convincingly landed odds of 1/2 at Newcastle.

The Saturday after York, Baileys Black Tie won his second race of the season, bringing the monthly tally to ten. Twenty-four hours later Royal Rebel took the Listed Ballycullen Stakes at Leopardstown over one mile six furlongs, after which Peter Savill announced that the horse's next race would be in the Stockholm Cup, part of a multiple Savill attack on that card. Unfortunately, the afternoon's other foreign raider, Ice, disappointed in Ovrevoll's Marit Sveaas Minnelop, finishing a distant fourth of twelve.

Generally the team continued to put the disappointment of York behind them. At Hamilton on the 24th, Break the Code eventually broke his duck at odds of 1/3, the narrow margin of his victory owing much, in Mark's opinion, to over confidence on Darryll Holland's part. Once again, a Prescott trained runner frustrated Johnston's ambitions, High Cheviot and Hayelah having to settle for places behind Kingdom of Gold in a mile maiden. However,

Hayelah was so highly strung that Mark was relieved to see both her and Joe Fanning arrive back in one piece and was more than satisfied with her debut run. St. Helensfield then ran encouragingly over a trip short of his best, dead-heating for third behind Mick Easterby's Jedi Knight.

At Goodwood on August 28th Yavana's Pace contested the Sport on Five March Stakes over one mile six furlongs. His four opponents included one of the St Leger favourites, Iscan, as well as Nowhere to Exit. Richard Hughes had the mount on Yavana's Pace and eventually won by half a length from Iscan. The press focused on Iscan's apparent bad luck in running, completely ignoring the fact that Yavana's Pace had only been ridden with hands and heels, and might well have been able to repel a more serious challenge had one been thrown down. Still, the plan to go to the Irish St Leger remained on course. Across at Newmarket, Kashra landed a valuable nursery under Michael Hills, justifying favouritism in the process, and confirming the dramatic improvement made since she had learned to settle. Meantime, at Redcar, Harryana returned from a long lay-off to win a five-furlongs conditions event.

Happy Change had his second outing of the month in another conditions race over ten-furlongs at Epsom on August 30th. In a tactical affair he made most before quickening away, holding on by a comfortable two and a half lengths from Muhib. Frustratingly for Mark, although the horse had just proved himself to be pretty useful, his owners, The Winning Line, had already arranged to collect him at Epsom so that he could be returned to Venetia Williams for a hurdling campaign. Even though he knew that this was part of their plan he was still disappointed to lose him at that particular moment. Left to him, he would have run the horse in the Group 3 September Stakes over the same course five days later, having been informed earlier in the day that insufficient entries had been received and that the race was to be re-opened.

To aggravate matters, the following morning The Winning Line asked Mark, who still held 'authority to act', to declare Happy Change after all. However, by this time Mark had persuaded John Keaney to allow him to enter Yavanna's Pace and felt obliged to refuse.

The curtain came down on another successful month via White Heart in Baden-Baden's Darley-Oettingen-Rennen (Group 3) over a mile on August 31st. John Reid brought the gelding home by a length from the Danish outsider Intruder and John Dunlop's Haami, the odds-on favourite.

August had seen a further 15 British winners, moving the overall total to 84 and ever closer to that century. Two winners abroad improved the foreign tally to six. The strike rate for August had once again been good (21.2%), moving the annual rate forward to 16.5%. British win prize money for the month totalled £88,632, making a running total of £490,765. Foreign win prize money for August was £38,795, bringing that haul to £249,719.

CHAPTER THIRTEEN

September 1999

The turf season begins to wind down in September. Evening racing becomes a thing of the past—a memory of balmy, high-summer nights—as harbingers of autumn, like the St Leger meeting, confront our senses. For a trainer, this time of the year presents difficult challenges. Almost inevitably the weather changes. Horses with form on a sound surface begin to struggle; horses needing soft ground are entered, only for their trainers to find that there are literally scores whose handlers have been waiting for exactly the same surface. Time begins to run out for those patiently awaiting the right race on the right going, and owners with horses yet to run often become full of angst. Races are found for previously unraced two-year-olds, strings begin to pull out in the morning in the dark. Additionally, the round of yearling sales gets under way. From Doncaster to Keeneland, from Keeneland to Goffs, from Goffs to Newmarket, the show rolls on. Catalogues and pedigrees require substantial research in advance and the yearlings themselves physical examination, detailed study and a good eye. For a yard the size of Kingsley House sales time is very demanding.

Johnston has very firm views about buying yearlings. First and foremost, he trusts his own judgement. Specialists may be brought in to assist with pedigrees or examination of x-rays and the like, but at the end of the day Johnston attends the sales personally, makes his selections personally and, finally, bids himself. It follows then that he does not deal with bloodstock agents, preferring the evidence of his own eyes to second-hand advice. The success of his purchases over the years speaks for itself, but there is a down side to his approach in that certain bloodstock agents undoubtedly have a major say in advising their clients on suitable training establishments. It is undeniable that every trainer seeks to have the highest possible quality of horse in his/her yard. But, in failing to establish close links with leading agents, Johnston runs the risk of prejudicing his chances of attracting even more quality horses; horses which are often directed to leading Newmarket yards instead.

A canny Scot, Mark is determined to obtain value for money. He is interested mainly in purchasing yearlings whose pedigrees have sufficient class to suggest that they might reasonably be expected to make into decent race-horses. Given this filtering criteria, more often than not he finds that better value for money lies in purchasing horses which have a staying pedigree. Current fashion and the leaning of some sales companies towards more pre-cocious types have forced up the asking price for that type of horse, and though Mark is more than happy to train the sharper type of animal, and indeed has enjoyed great success in doing so, he is not happy about gambling on a horse being something of a freak to improve upon the potential of its pedigree. Perhaps it goes some way to explaining why the public perception of him as a trainer of stayers exists. Of course, a certain Double Trigger might also have influenced the racing public too! Mark sums up his attitude to the sales when he says: "I am determined to do my utmost to obtain value for money for my owners and to attempt to fill my yard with as high a class of horse as possible within the funds available to me."

With regard to September, the range of winners enjoyed by Kingsley House in recent years had varied between five (in 1994) and fifteen (in 1998). Given its good run of form through July and August, the yard was well on course for its target of one-hundred but, all the same, a minimum of ten winners was wanted this particular month to keep the pot boiling.

The main early skirmishes took place on Saturday, the 4th, when Yavana's Pace contested the Group 3 Victor Chandler September Stakes at Epsom, whilst Gaelic Storm tackled exalted company in the Group 1 Stanley Leisure Sprint Cup at Haydock Park.

As Yavana's Pace was to be saddled at Epsom by Brendan Holland, Mark, accompanied by yours truly, travelled to Haydock. There, the hope had been that "normal" going conditions for the course in September would be encountered and that Gaelic Storm might, in fact, get his favoured soft ground. In the event, not only was the ground good to firm, it was also a glorious day, fine for a shirt-sleeved crowd and for the pilot of the microlight aircraft parked on the infield of the course, but more than a little disappointing to the gelding's connections. Heading the market at 13/8 was Godolphin's Diktat, who was unbeaten in 1999, having lifted the Dubai Sports Shergar Cup Seven at Goodwood, the Van Geest Criterion Stakes at Newmarket and the Group 1 Prix Maurice de Gheest at Deauville. Next, at 4/1, was Luca Cumani's Arkadian Hero and only two others of a sixteen-strong field started at odds shorter than 10/1. Gaelic Storm, who went off at 50/1, was outpaced on the firm ground through the first part of the race before keeping on to finish tenth, only five lengths or so behind the winner who, predictably enough, was Diktat. Given the conditions, a most creditable performance.

Gaelic Storm's race was at 3 pm. This allowed us time to make our way to the owners and trainers bar for a beer and a sandwich before installing ourselves in front of a television to watch Yavana's Pace and Joe Fanning at Epsom. In his column in the *Racing Post* that morning, Mark had attacked the press for rubbishing Yavana's Pace's victory over Iscan at Goodwood. He made it clear that the horse was in high form and warned punters to "ignore Yavana's Pace at your peril".

Confidence was high. Earlier that morning Deirdre had expressed the view that she thought Yavana's Pace better over a mile and a half, the distance of the Epsom race, rather than the mile and three quarters of Goodwood. Young Charlie Johnston, after studying the *Post*, pronounced that the race was at Yavana's mercy. Whilst Mark had been happy to give Joe Fanning the ride he was a little concerned that the camber of the Epsom course might not suit his style. Johnson reckoned the jockey still needed to improve his use of the whip in his left hand and wondered whether, if Yavana's Pace rolled towards the fence, would he be able to drive him with his whip in that hand.

Blueprint, with Kieren Fallon on board, was all the rage and, in fairness, the horse had beaten Yavana's Pace comfortably in Newmarket's Fred Archer Stakes at the end of June. So it wasn't surprising that he started odds on, Yavana's Pace lengthening from 5/2 to 11/4. Given the latter's history of pre-race antics, Mark's first concern was to establish that the partnership had arrived at the start intact. Frustratingly, Channel 4's pictures seemed deliberately to avoid showing the horse, but when the camera angle finally switched to a view of the stalls immediately before the off, he was reassured that they were both safely there.

Fanning soon had the gelding settled behind the leaders, going well. Rounding Tattenham Corner Mark urged him to wait, concerned that he might make for home just too early. Understandably, perhaps, Joe went a shade early and, momentarily, it looked as though Mark's fears about his use of the whip might be well founded as Yavana's Pace began to roll about under pressure. Fortunately, though, the gelding had the measure of Blueprint, and as Yavana's Pace crossed the line Mark slapped me on the back saying excitedly: "That was Joe Fanning's first Group winner." There was no mistaking his delight, not just for training a winner, but even more so for the landmark in Fanning's career. The County Wicklow born twenty-nine-year old has been around for ages and deserved his break into the top echelons of the riding profession. Mark remains convinced there is work to be done on his riding style but, as this race confirmed, Joe seems well equipped for the challenge. To cap everything, he is a charming and polite man.

A second success was recorded at Hamilton on September 6th, when Maktoum al Maktoum's Cadeaux Genereux colt Golden Miracle finally got his head in front in a six-furlong nursery. It had been hoped that he might have achieved more by this stage of the season but, better late than never. The next day, at Leicester, the four-year-old gelding Darwell's Folly, in first-time blinkers, belatedly did his bit too.

On September 8th, Kashra tackled listed company in the Sirenia Stakes at Kempton. Unfortunately, this time she reverted to her old ways, refusing to settle and was a spent force inside the final furlong. In fairness, the first two, Primo Valentino and Seazun, ended the season amongst the leading juveniles, so fourth place wasn't exactly a disgrace in the circumstances.

The St Leger meeting at Doncaster saw a number of the stable's leading lights in action. On Thursday the 9th, White Heart kicked off the Kingsley House challenge in the GNER Park Stakes (Group 3) over a mile. However, a 25/1 shot, he had only average prospects at best, and was not helped when John Reid (recently contracted to ride for Maktoum al Maktoum's Gainsborough Stud operation) found himself short of room at a crucial stage. Hiddnah was next to challenge, Johnston being more than hopeful of her chances in the Group 3 May Hill Stakes. Eleven potentially smart fillies opposed her, including Peter Chapple-Hyam's Princess Ellen, winner of the Sweet Solera Stakes at Newmarket in mid-August, and John Dunlop's Caerleon filly Aunty Rose, the winner of her only race to date, a Newmarket maiden at the end of July. Hiddnah was unable to land a blow, eventually staying on steadily for fifth, giving the impression that she now needed further. Joe Mercer's immediate post-race reaction was that she should be put away and trained with an eye to the Oaks next season.

Before the Doncaster Cup, Double Trigger paraded before the stands. Additionally, a presentation took place in the parade ring, where Mark was given by a plaque the marketing manager of GNER commemorating the naming of the engine. Double Trigger was absolutely full of himself and looked in great order. This was the first time Mark had seen him since he'd left the yard to go to stud, and when interviewed over the PA system his genuine affection for him came across strongly. The racecard portrayed "Trigger" on the cover and also dedicated a full page tribute to "an equine hero". The tone of that summed up the regard in which he is held: "Northern racegoers know and appreciate a good horse when they see one; Double Trigger was more than that—he was a champion. We welcome back the conquering hero."

Unfortunately Johnston's three subsequent runners all failed to make an impact and later at the St Leger Yearling Sales he seemed in downbeat mood. "A bad day at the office" was how he summed up the day's racing. There, in company with his fellow directors' daughter, Susie Palmer, he looked at a number of horses before concluding that he had seen nothing "about which I could get excited" and heading home. Interestingly, in the light of subsequent events, our conversation that evening also touched upon Mark's concerns regarding certain aspects of the conduct of bloodstock sales in Britain. He declared himself a fan of the American system where he feels faster selling and bidding and a healthier attitude to the disclosure of vices encourages greater confidence amongst purchasers.

The following day got off to a better start, Mardani making a bold bid to land the Mallard Stakes over an extended mile and three quarters. Clearly relishing firmer underfoot conditions than he'd encountered in the Ebor, he beat all but Sean Woods's Knockholt. Later on, Dramatic Quest took up the challenge in the Frigidaire Champagne Stakes (Group 2), the field also including Barry Hills's Distant Music, Marcus Tregoning's Ekraar and Aidan O'Brien's Rossini, all potentially smart colts. Sent off at 8/1, Dramatic Quest ran as though needing further and, sensibly, Holland was easy on him once it became clear he would not reach the frame. Despite finishing fifth, hopes remain high that he'll develop into a top-class three-year-old. However, in the concluding sprint handicap, Lady Melbourne ran poorly.

The stable's runners on St Leger day itself comprised the handicappers Alberich and Robin Lane and the two year old fillies Fez and Harryana. Both Alberich and Robin Lane acquitted themselves with great credit in competitive events, the former leading three furlongs from home before giving best to the joint-favourites, Musician and King Alex. Robin Lane was probably unlucky. Back to her front-running best, she defied all bar Amalia, who bumped her before nosing ahead inside the final 100 yards. She finished second of seventeen, beaten one and a quarter lengths.

Fez and Harryana looked to hold fair prospects in a competitive Flying Childers Stakes (Group 2). Fez, sent off the 9/2 joint-favourite with Tim Easterby's Buy or Sell, ran in typically brave fashion before, frustratingly, getting beaten two heads and a neck into fourth. Harryana ran poorly. You will recall Mark and I having to remove sheep from the High Moor turf gallop to allow Fez to work the previous Saturday. Perhaps we should have let her clear her own!

A poorish Doncaster, then, even though some (notably on the Saturday), gave the stable hope for the future. Pleasingly, before anyone became too downcast, Star Rage returned to winning form at Goodwood over two miles, quickening well for Jason Weaver to win his nineteenth race with the minimum of fuss.

Peter Savill's 'raid on Taby' took place on September 12th. Johnston's pair of Acicula and Royal Rebel were joined there by David (Dandy) Nicholls' Proud Native, a good third in the Nunthorpe Stakes behind Stravinsky and Robert Collet's Sainte Marine. Proud Native duly won the Taby Open Sprint Championship but Acicula didn't appear to enjoy the experience of running on dirt, finishing only eighth in a listed race over a mile. Royal Rebel also failed to repeat his Leopardstown running for Dean McKeown in the Group 3

Stockholm Cup International, the race being won by Albaran, the Norwegian-based horse who had beaten Yavana's Pace at Klampenborg.

Closer to home, Markus Graff's Prince of Birds colt Cool Investment made a winning debut at Musselburgh on the 13th under Joe Fanning and, forty-eight hours later, Maktoum al Maktoum's Kind Regards was successful in the maiden fillies stakes at Beverley for Darryll Holland. Both added to a now impressive statistic of two-year-old winners/horses to have raced, currently standing at 50%.

Paradise Garden returned to the fray at Newbury on September 17th in the Haynes, Hanson and Clark Conditions Stakes over a mile. Again he shaped like a stayer, making the running before keeping on strongly to take second behind an impressive winner in Ethmaar, from Marcus Tregoning's in-form stable. The following day, at Ayr, it was decided to let Gaelic Storm take his chance in the Gold Cup despite the fact that he'd 9 st 9 lb to carry. Poorly drawn in stall 3 (the first four home were drawn 17, 28, 18 and 21), he ran a stormer, finishing strongly, at the line a close eighth of twenty-eight. The only two above him in the handicap, Ho-Leng and Eastern Purple, finished twenty-sixth and twenty-eighth respectively.

The yard's two other runners at Ayr that day performed lamentably. Kashra disappointed first in the Firth of Clyde Stakes, again running too freely, eventually finishing last of six whilst Ice, so impressive early in the season, took the same position in a nineteen-runner handicap over a mile. Thankfully, things went far better at Newbury where Alberich, humping 9 st 12 lb in the Tote Sporting Index Autumn Cup over an extended one mile five furlongs, was given an excellent ride by Royston Ffrench, dictating a steady pace before quickening to hold off all-comers up the straight. His connections were understandably delighted at landing an excellent prize of £18,400.

Ffrench had been offered the ride because Darryll Holland was on duty at Ayr for Gaelic Storm and Joe Fanning was otherwise engaged in Ireland, partnering Yavana's Pace in the Irish St Leger at the Curragh. Unlike the oldest British Classic (which remains for three-year-olds only), the Irish authorities decided some years ago to open up their equivalent to older horses. Though this decision was roundly criticised at the time it has undeniably improved the quality of the race. The 1999 renewal attracted a field of just five, all high-class horses. In addition to Yavana's Pace, Aidan O' Brien's three-year-old Genghis Khan, a winner at the Curragh and Leopardstown earlier in the year; John Oxx's Enzeli, the winner of the latest Ascot Gold Cup for HH the Aga Khan; John Dunlop's St Leger winner Silver Patriarch, and Godolphin's Kayf Tara, winner of the 1998 renewal and fresh from recent victories in the Goodwood Cup and the Prix Kergorlay at Deauville. Kayf Tara was sent off 1/2 favourite, followed by Silver Patriarch and Enzeli, both at 5/1. Yavana's Pace started at 7/1 but Genghis Khan, at 25/1, was largely ignored.

Yavana's Pace ran a cracker, settling in third, improving entering the straight then unable to match Kayf Tara's change of pace. The way Yavana's Pace hung left throughout the final two furlongs once again reminded me of Mark's comments regarding Joe's use of the whip in his left hand. Despite that, the gelding maintained a sufficiently strong gallop to take second, eleven lengths clear of Silver Patriarch and a further five clear of Enzeli. Tentative plans had been made to send Yavana's Pace to Australia for the Melbourne Cup in early November; after this effort they were finalised.

The abandonment of Ascot's prestige card on September 25th was unfortunate as, had the track been raceable, Gaelic Storm would have relished the underfoot conditions and held a big chance in a valuable seven-furlong handicap. Although the feature races were transferred to the Sunday, that one was lost altogether. Still, Robin Lane kept the flag flying with a brave display in the Ritz Club Stakes (worth £46,300 to the winner), leading until the final furlong before being overhauled by Vicious Circle, the Ebor winner, and two others.

At least Musselburgh yielded a winner. There, Mr and Mrs Gary Middlebrook's tough old stick Etterby Park, last seen out at Chester on July 25th, returned with a vengeance to land the Jolly Farmer Handicap over two miles. Afterwards, the gelding was once again targeted for the Cesarewitch at Newmarket on October 16th, a race also mapped out for last year's winner Spirit of Love and the lightly-raced Sinon.

On the continent Akbar and Mardani contested the Grand Prix Jockey Club at Dielsdorf, in Switzerland. However, in that they came accross a smart French horse in Trait de Genie, who duly landed the spoils from Akbar to record his third straight success in this race.

Hamilton's meeting on the 27th provided a further success when Golden Miracle took another nursery (Tote Hamilton Park Two Year Old Final) at the expense of his stable-companion Glenwhargen, who was turning in a much improved performance after three months off.

Newcastle is one of Johnston's favourite tracks, and its final September fixture saw three interesting performances. In the six-furlong two-year-old maiden, Mana d'Argent improved markedly on his debut to finish third whilst Champfis, an Efisio colt introduced in the same race, also performed with some credit. So far as Mark was concerned, though, High Cheviot's performance was the most encouraging. He relished the test of stamina posed by conditions (a mile on soft ground) in the maiden to score more comfortably for Darryll Holland than his winning margin of half a length suggested.

At the end of September, Johnston was satisfied with a monthly return of 10, which increased his cumulative total of British winners for the year to 94, tantalisingly close to the century. Win prize money in Britain now stood at £573,966.

CHAPTER FOURTEEN

October 1999

At the outset of October there was no doubt whatsoever where the focus of the stable's attentions lay: Fruits of Love's challenge for the Canadian International (Grade 1) at Woodbine on October 17th. After all, the target of a yearly Group 1 win for Kingsley House remained outstanding, 'Fruity's' third in the King George and Yavana's Pace's second in the Irish St Leger the nearest they'd come. After Canada, the plan was to then take 'Fruity' to Gulfstream Park for the Breeders' Cup Turf three weeks later and to round off his season in the Japan Cup, in which, surely, he could expect to get firm ground.

In the meantime, there were several big meetings on home soil, notably at Newmarket. Alas, neither of the stable's runners, Let It Rain and St Helensfield, landed a blow in the Tote Cambridgeshire on October 2nd and Harryana failed to sparkle in Redcar's NTL Two Year Old Trophy on the same day, though in fairness she probably didn't stay six furlongs. Despite a gallant effort from Champfis at Catterick, beaten less than a length in a five-furlong maiden, the yard was winnerless until that tough filly Caerosa popped up at 20/1 in an apprentice handicap at York on the 7th.

When meeting Mark on Saturday the 9th, he told me that Fruits of Love was well and would fly out to Canada from Heathrow later that day. Yavana's Pace would leave for Melbourne on the Monday and would be accompanying Kayf Tara. He also pointed out that Fruits of Love would not now contest the Breeders' Cup Turf, travel costs from Canada being exorbitant. To run in that, Mick Doyle would have to pay $40,000 to transport Fruits of Love from Ontario to Florida plus $40,000 in entry fees and a further $35,000 to transport the colt back to New York. Given those costs, and reflecting on the probability that Fruits of Love would be more likely to give of his best in Japan, it seemed to them both that the sensible option was to allow the horse maximum recovery time between Woodbine and Japan.

Later on the 9th, at York, Johnston ran Kayo, owned by David Abell. Formerly trained by Tim Etherington, the gelding hadn't run since finishing well down the field at Southwell on July 24th and shaped most encouragingly under Michael Roberts on his return, finishing fifth of twenty-two in the hotly-contested Coral Sprint Trophy.

At last, a second victory of the month, Darwell's Folly popping up on the all-weather at Wolverhampton on the 13th. Mind you, the gelding, dropped to claiming class, required hard riding by Darryll Holland to justify favouritism.

Redcar on the 14th saw the two-year-old College Chapel filly, Footprints, fail narrowly to land a median auction race. However, Kayo made amends in a seven-furlong handicap later on the card, seeing off a mammoth field easily.

As the stable's century loomed it seemed fitting that Gaelic Storm got in on the act again. Relishing good to soft ground at Newmarket on October 15th he came out best in the Bedford Lodge Hotel Bentinck Stakes, produced with the proverbial wet sail by Darryll Holland inside the final furlong.

In the following day's Cesarewitch Johnston was three-handed with Sinon, Spirit of Love and Etterby Park. Mark had made fairly positive noises about

Sinon during a televised interview at the course and each-way punters seemed to latch on to him, fuelled by John McCririck singling the Ela Mana Mou colt out as a market mover on *The Morning Line*. However, injury had kept him off the course for well over a year and it remained to be seen whether the gradual build-up in his work schedule would equip him to deal with such a competitive handicap on his return to the fray. Darryll Holland took the ride. Etterby Park was also expected to run well but, in Spirit of Love's case, Mark was just hopeful, the horse having continued to endure a series of niggling problems and been absent from the track since the Gold Cup. However, if back on song, his chances were obvious.

In the event, none of the trio shone, although Etterby Park and Spirit of Love did race prominently for a long way. Sinon appeared not to stay and Darryll Holland was not hard on him when it became apparent that he was not going to be involved in the finish. Late-season foreign targets now awaited both Sinon and Spirit of Love and it remained to be seen whether Holland's tender handling of the former would pay dividends.

Mark was to fly to Canada immediately after racing at Newmarket and Kayo's win in the closing seven-furlong handicap sent him off in high spirits. Once again the gelding pulled away from a large field, leaving the distinct impression he was good enough to follow up.

Toronto's Woodbine Raceway, "the racetrack of the future", is host to the Canadian International, a Grade 1 event run over one and a half miles on the EP Taylor Turf course (named after the breeder of the legendary Northern Dancer). Although the original course opened in 1874 on what was then the far eastern suburbs of Toronto the present circuit, opened in June 1956, is situated on 750 acres on the north western outskirts of the city, close to the Lester B. Pearson International Airport. The track has undergone several multi-million dollar expansions and upgrades and is now regarded as one of the world's premier racecourses, having staged the Breeders' Cup in 1996.

The three most important races run there are the Queen's Plate, North America's oldest continuously run Stakes race, the Woodbine Mile, carrying a guaranteed prize fund of $500,000 and the Canadian International itself. The Queen's Plate was first run in 1860 and in 1997 Her Majesty the Queen visited the course to witness that year's renewal and to present the trophy. The Woodbine Mile replaced the Woodbine Million and is just one of a lucrative autumn schedule of valuable turf races at the track, including the Grade 1 EP Taylor Stakes over ten furlongs, a race which is often a target for European raiders. The course also hosts the Breeders' Stakes, one leg of the Canadian Triple Crown, completed by the Queen's Plate and the Prince of Wales Stakes run at Fort Erie.

The status currently enjoyed by the Canadian International was assured in the seventies when no fewer than five of its winners earned an Eclipse award as North American grass horse of the year. Dahlia, Snow Knight, Youth and MacDiarmida were preceded by "Big Red", the great Secretariat in 1973, who clinched his championship in his farewell to racing at Woodbine. In fairness, given earlier remarks about Royal Anthem, the 1998 renewal saw a great performance by that colt who made all to defeat the 1997 Breeders' Cup Turf winner Chief Bearhart.

The latest running attracted horses bred in Canada, USA, Brazil, Ireland, Chile and England, all seeking a first prize of $936,000 (from total stakes of $1.56m). There were three British-trained challengers, Fruits of Love being joined by Paul Cole's lightly raced four-year-old Generous colt, Courteous, (fresh from a win in the Grand Prix de Deauville) and Bienamado, a three-year-old colt by Bien Bien, now owned by Canadians John Toffan and Trudy McCaffery but trained at Manton by George Foster. Last time out the latter had run extremely well against Montjeu, going down narrowly in the Prix Niel. After the sensational sacking of Peter Chapple-Hyam by Manton's owner Robert Sangster in August, Foster had been put in temporary charge and this trip was clearly very important to him.

The American-based challengers comprised Tanaasa, formerly with Sir Michael Stoute; Gritty Sandie, supplemented into the race after a win in a Grade 3 handicap at Belmont in September; Dancing Place, a multiple Group winner in his native Chile but, like Tanaasa, now trained in California by Neil Drysdale, for whom he had finished second in the Grade 2 Del Mar handicap in August; and the Brazilian-bred rank outsider, Beautiful Dancer.

The home team fielded two Woodbine-based runners, Joe Strizl's four-year-old Dawson's Legacy, the Canadian champion two-year-old in 1997, and Phil England's Thornfield, a son of the 1991 International winner Sky Classic out of Alexandrina, a daughter of the 1985 Queen's Plate winner, La Lorgnette. Thornfield thus was attempting to become the first horse to follow in his sire's footsteps.

Kieren Fallon replaced Olivier Peslier on Fruits of Love. Prior to the race Johnston described the colt's preparation to Canada's *Thoroughbred Today* as follows:- "He's had a long break since his last run but that was a deliberate move to bring him to Woodbine fresh. We've been planning since very early in the year that he would come here. We've learned the hard way after some failures travelling overseas and feel quite strongly that the way to bring a horse on a long trip is to arrive fresh and not do too much work once here. He's coming into the race in perfect shape and ready to run. He'll be taking things pretty easy leading up to it, just steady cantering and nothing fast. We'll be saving the main event for Sunday. He's been working up to the full mile and a half. We took him to a racecourse (Pontefract) for a spin about three weeks ago when we were a bit concerned about his weight. He was 512 kilos and we were looking for 500 but he worked a mile and a half and didn't lose even a pound, so clearly it didn't take anything out of him. He's an impressive horse to look at but laid back and lazy in training. He has to be shaken up to do anything in training but is coming into this race in tip-top condition."

Interestingly, *Thoroughbred Today*'s pre-race "Contender Profile" on Fruits of Love seemed to acknowledge a lack of regard for his previous achievements by sections of the media and the racing public. After a brief discussion of his motorway accident it stated: "Despite adversity Fruits of Love has gone on to a world-class career with very little respect. When he won last year's Princess of Wales's Stakes at Newmarket he was a 7/1 long shot. When he won the Dubai Turf Classic again he was an outsider and when he defeated Royal Anthem to win the Hardwicke Stakes at Royal Ascot he was still dismissed by the public at 12/1. In Sunday's race, the son of Hansel will take on an unfamiliar role as one of the race favourites … but one subject the Virginia-bred knows very well is how to win!"

In truth, this race seemed to provide the perfect opportunity for Fruits of Love to achieve a Group 1 success for the stable. Deirdre had flown out to Canada the week before to partner him on his spins around Woodbine. Mark was to follow after Saturday's racing at Newmarket (this being the week of the Tattersalls' Newmarket October Yearling Sales, Europe's largest and arguably most informative yearling auction). Johnston was quietly confident, especially with the North American style of racing likely to produce the strong early pace which his stable star required. Only the going on Woodbine's turf course gave cause for concern. Rain during the week preceding the race led to the ground being officially stated as good. In a perfect world, Fruits of Love would have preferred a firmer racing surface. Nonetheless the Yorkshire-trained horse was sent off an 18/10 favourite in a nine-strong field.

In the event, Fruits of Love just failed to land the spoils, defied by the Woodbine-based horse, Thornfield. As things turned out, the result hung on the performance of the principal jockeys and the luck in running enjoyed by their respective mounts. Rick Dos Ramos on the winner was able to track the leader, Courteous, expending minimum effort in so doing. Dos Ramos commented: "Phil England decided who the two or three speed horses were and that we should get a good position. I stayed on the fence the whole way and had a good trip with him. That front runner tried to sprint clear but couldn't, so I was in good shape because I still hadn't asked Thornfield to really run. We mowed him down in the stretch." Kieren Fallon on the other hand enjoyed considerably less success in attempting to execute his battle plan. The pace set by Courteous was steady and, consequently, the remainder of the nine-strong field bunched behind the leader approaching the home turn. Caught up in some general tightening which ensued, Fallon found his mount shuffled back to last at the top of the turn. From thereon it was unlikely that Fruits of Love would prevail, despite a brave, late rally which took him to within a length of the winner. Fallon's view was that the horse needed firmer ground and would have quickened much better granted such. Mark was bitterly disappointed, commenting to the *Racing Post*'s North American correspondent Dan Farley: "I think the horse was in the right form but just wasn't in a winning position turning for home." He felt that his charge really ought to have won and subsequently expressed the view to me that he felt Kieren Fallon knew that too. Writing in his column on October 23rd Johnston summed up his feelings thus: "I don't mean to be disrespect-ful to any of our opposition—it was a decent Group 1 race—but I thought beforehand that Fruits of Love should win. If my judgement was correct and I had prepared him properly for the race, I believed he would do it. The Canadian International was his best chance to date. Most things were in his favour, although we would have preferred the ground a little faster. I couldn't help but feel that, if the race had been run a little differently, he would have won it."

Pain of defeat was eased somewhat by the six world series points earned and also by the handsome second place prize money of £117,188, making this the second most remunerative race of the horse's career. Although disap-pointed, Johnston confirmed that Fruits of Love would take his place in the line-up for the Japan Cup on November 28th.

Despite odds of 19/1, Thornfield was a popular winner locally as his owner, Steve Stavro, 72, is Chairman, Governor and owner of the Toronto Maple

Leafs, one of the premier ice hockey clubs in the world. Asked how this Grade 1 success compared to a Leafs victory in the Stanley Cup, Stavro confessed: "the Cup would be a little better, but it'd be close!"

Back in England, second seemed the order of the day. Paradise Garden, contesting the Tote Bookmakers' Silver Tankard Stakes (Listed) at Pontefract on October 18th, failed by a neck to resist the determined challenge of Hataab. The following day, another of David Abell's two-year-olds, an Efisio filly called Branston Fizz, made her debut at Lingfield, shaping with great promise behind John Dunlop's colt Don't Surrender, the pair five lengths clear of the third horse. However, a welcome change of luck came twenty-four hours later at Gosforth Park when Kayo justified favouritism in a competitive sprint handicap. Even more significant, however, was the performance of Abell's Virgin Soldier, a three-year-old Waajib gelding previously in the care of Tim Etherington, who made his debut for the stable in a twenty-runner ten-furlong handicap on the same card. An enterprising ride from Joe Fanning almost paid off, the partnership collared by the favourite only inside the final furlong. Virgin Soldier never looked back from that point onwards, improving by leaps and bounds. Nonetheless, bar Kayo, the bout of "seconditis" continued until Awake ran out an impressive winner of a Newbury nursery on October 23rd.

At Lingfield, just five days after his debut for the yard, Virgin Soldier confirmed the promise of that Newcastle run by winning under Royston Ffrench. A cross-country double for the stable was achieved the following day when, firstly, Fanning gave an exhibition of patient hands and heels riding to nurse Footprints home in a median auction maiden at Redcar then, later that afternoon at Bath, Darryll Holland overcame trouble in running to score on Caerosa.

As the month drew to a close, Inca Star, a colt by Trempolino, made a promising debut in a mile maiden for two-year-olds at Yarmouth. Desperately green, he took an age to find his stride, belatedly powering home into third, in the process defeating several more experienced and better fancied runners. Definitely one for the future, was Mark's reaction.

For a while Johnston had been planning a two-pronged attack on one of his favourite races, Newmarket's Zetland Stakes (Listed) on Saturday October 30th. In the end High Cheviot and Paradise Garden did duty, the latter starting 4/1 joint favourite in a ten-strong field. However, High Cheviot failed to give his running at all, eventually finishing eighth. Paradise Garden was soon up with the pace, but the combination of softish ground and an extreme distance for two-year-olds (10f) appeared to be too much and he laboured home a weary fourth. Still, at least some compensation was gained when Windy Gulch took advantage of a favourable draw in the concluding seven-furlong handicap, in the process recording her fourth success of the season.

Despite the disappointment in Canada, the October statistics made acceptable reading. Eleven domestic winners were achieved at a monthly strike rate of 12.0%, moving the yearly figure to 15.2%. Additionally, it was only three short of the yard's best ever haul for October, which had been achieved during Johnston's *annus mirabilis* of 1994. Win prize money in Britain now totalled £640,763 and foreign win prize money remained at £249,719. The British win and place prize money at the end of the month was creeping ever closer to the target figure of £1m, (these figures excluding Fruits of Love's Woodbine reward of £117,000!).

CHAPTER FIFTEEN

November 1999

November 2nd saw the 139th renewal of the Melbourne Cup, run at Flemington, Victoria. Six years previously Vintage Crop, trained by Dermot Weld in Ireland, had triumphed sensationally in Australia's greatest race, a victory which prefaced a regular challenge from European horses in subsequent seasons. As already noted, Johnston had tried twice before, with Quick Ransom and Double Trigger. Neither was able to emulate Vintage Crop, Quick Ransom finishing 23rd in 1994 and Double Trigger 18th in 1995. Still, valuable lessons had been learned from those defeats and, given the improvement shown by Yavana's Pace, Mark persuaded his owners, John and Joan Keaney, to let the horse take his chance. Incidentally, Quick Ransom subsequently remained in Australia to be trained by Lee Freeman. He ran in the race again in 1995, finishing a close fourth. In Mark's view the 1994 scenario had been a case of the right horse with the wrong preparation—he was determined Yavana's Pace would receive the correct one this time.

'The Cup' was first run in 1861. According to legend, its first winner, Archer, was reported to have walked 850 km from Nowra to Flemington in order to contest the race. Dramatically, one of the runners, Twilight, bolted and was captured only after he'd completed the whole course. Two others, Dispatch and Medora died after falls.

Archer retained his crown the following year, his grateful owners having pampered him this time by shipping him to Flemington, but his bid to land a hat-trick of wins was foiled by officialdom. Due to postal delays his nomination to race failed to arrive in time. The authorities, in turn, refused to allow the horse to compete. Such was the disgust at their action that, in a show of solidarity, many owners scratched their horses from the race. A field of seven in 1863 remains the smallest ever to contest the Melbourne Cup. How interesting that, even in nineteenth century Australia, racing's authorities seem to have been out of step with public opinion!

In 1861, Archer's owners received £710 and a 'hand beaten' gold watch by way of a prize. A crowd of some 4,000 watched the race. By 1999, the winner's prize money had multiplied to £677,122 (even the fifth-placed horse earns £29,520) and the Victoria Racing Club looked forward to a crowd of up to 100,000 people at Flemington. Not bad for a stayers' handicap!

The VRC and the race sponsors, Foster's Lager, market the Cup as the horserace which stops a nation. "It may not officially be our national day of celebration" states the VRC web-site, "but unofficially it is." Quite literally, the entire country grinds to a halt for the running of the race. Parties and barbecues are held everywhere to celebrate the day and, at Flemington itself, the crowds start arriving at 8am to savour the atmosphere of the occasion in full, boot parties being the order of the day in the members' car park.

Entertainment is laid on throughout the day, with massed bands, aerobatic fly-pasts, fashion competitions, celebrities singing "Waltzing Matilda" and the like. As post time approaches the jockeys are introduced to the crowd in the mounting yard. Excitement rises to fever pitch as the stalls open, continuing throughout the race. Anyone who has witnessed the successful horse and jockey returning to the winner's enclosure will have been struck by the special atmosphere Cup day engenders.

Johnston was confident that lessons learned from Quick Ransom and Double Trigger's participation would help him to produce a better performance from Yavana's Pace. Nevertheless, the logistical problems encountered in running a horse on the other side of the world remain considerable. For starters, quarantine arrangements require to be made, both before departure and upon arrival in the host country. Transport costs are phenomenal, flights lengthy, jockey arrangements complicated and expensive, staffing costly and communication difficult. Even feed and bedding can be problematic. Acclimatisation of the horse can never be taken for granted. However, Yavana's Pace and his lass Hayley Brough eventually travelled with Godolphin's pair, Kayf Tara and Central Park, and James Fanshawe's Travelmate on a twenty-seven hour flight from Heathrow to Melbourne on October 11th. Their arrival was greeted by a huge press contingent, including all of Australia's national television stations, their racing channel, at least six commercial radio stations and all the daily papers. Hayley was upbeat about Yavana's Pace's wellbeing after the journey. The four English horses were then dispatched to quarantine at Sandown Racecourse.

Back at base, Mark was in consultation with the owners about who should ride Yavana's Pace. His usual 'attention to detail' in his approach to such matters led him to reflect hard upon which jockey would maximise the horse's chance of winning. Yavana's Pace was known to give trouble in parades and when going to the start and Mark reckoned experience of Australian conditions was a significant advantage. For this reason in particular, he offered the ride to Richard Hughes, despite the fact that he had partnered Yavana's Pace only once before, when winning the March Stakes at Goodwood in August. Richard had previously had spells in Australia as an apprentice, with Peter Miles and Johnny Morris, and apart from having sixty rides under his belt knew Flemington fairly well.

Mark learned that Darryll Holland was not happy to have been passed over. As for Joe Fanning, who had ridden the horse to victory in the September Stakes and second place in the Irish St Leger, Mark commented: "If Yavana's Pace stays in training I am sure there will be no shortage of rides on him in the future for Joe. I have the greatest respect for Joe and I hope he is still heading for the top. But he has just one Group win under his belt and the Melbourne Cup is a quite exceptional race, requiring a huge amount of experience at that level."

The lead-up for the British trained horses proved eventful, to say the least. Firstly, Kayf Tara, the ante-post favourite, was found to have damaged the suspensory ligament in his near-fore. Godolphin's chief vet, Dr Mike Hauser, was flown from Dubai to examine the extent of the damage and a decision was taken six days prior to the race that the five year old would not run. Central Park, last seen out (when run off his feet) in the Juddmonte International Stakes at York in August, and previously last in the Coronation Cup, had been flown to Australia as travelling companion and lead horse for Kayf Tara. At that stage he was a possible runner in the Louis Vuitton Mackinnon Stakes (Grade 1) over ten furlongs at Flemington on the Saturday before the Cup. However, following Kayf Tara's defection, and keen to have a runner in the big race itself, Sheikh Mohammed gave the order that Central Park should be switched.

James Fanshawe's Travelmate was also well fancied, his whole campaign having been planned with Flemington in mind. Jockey Ray Cochrane, who had steered Lady Herries' Taufan's Melody to an historic but controversial success in the 1998 Caulfield Cup, had been instrumental in persuading connections that the horse was an ideal type and was confident of a big run. Indeed, when second to Vicious Circle in the Ebor, Travelmate had finished a long way ahead of Yavana's Pace. However, when legged up by Mick Easterby on Dancing Phantom in a mile and a half handicap at Doncaster on October 23rd, Cochrane could not have imagined the international bureaucratic farce which was to follow.

Under a typically enterprising and imaginative ride, Dancing Phantom had proved a clear-cut winner. Unfortunately, his jockey fell foul of the stewards, who spotted trouble in running in the early stages. As a result, Cochrane was suspended for two days for careless riding. Such bans start nine days after an offence is committed and, on that basis, Cochrane was ruled out of the Melbourne race. However, given that minor suspensions do not apply on days featuring Group 1 races, Racing Victoria were hopeful that the Jockey Club would allow Cochrane to ride. The Australian officials insisted that a two-day ban should run over successive days, but were prepared to allow the relevant days to be Sunday/Monday, thus freeing Cochrane to ride on Tuesday November 2nd, Cup day. After taking legal advice, however, the Jockey Club felt obliged to abide by the nine-day rule, meaning that Cochrane's ban had to start on Monday November 1st. They faxed Racing Victoria a copy of the Rules of Racing showing that exemptions to minor bans applied only when a Group 1 race was being run in Britain. Eventually, Cochrane was replaced by Hong Kong-based David Harrison, who was in many ways the ideal substitute, having ridden Travelmate to three successes when stable jockey to Fanshawe.

Interestingly, Greg Nichols of Racing Victoria commented on the affair that "the Jockey Club offered us the chance to break the conventions and said we could vary the rule (by allowing Cochrane to ride) and there wouldn't be any repercussions. But we've had enough controversies already and we feel we should stick to the rules." If this quotation is an accurate reflection of Nichols' comments, one wonders whom it was within the Jockey Club that made the offer of such a dispensation? Imagine the outcry from the Australian press if a banned jockey, especially Cochrane, who'd been suspended for a month after his ride in the Caulfield Cup in 1998, had won their great race? Many Australian racing professionals appear to hold near-xenophobic views about the modern trend of overseas runners contesting their major races, in particular Colin Alderson, President of the Australian Trainers' Association and trainer of the favourite, Sky Heights. Last year he had called for a limit on the number of overseas horses allowed to contest the Cup. Now he argued for overseas qualifying races to be held for potential international contenders, just as local horses must pre-qualify. "Tell them if they are not qualified, don't bother coming" he ranted, clearly still riled at the decision of the local racing authorities to eliminate one of his horses from the '98 Caulfield Cup to make way for Taufan's Melody (and Cochrane) who had failed to meet the initial qualification criteria for that race. He went on to call the 1999 challengers "B grade"! One wonders just what kind of qualifying races Alderson had in mind; Kayf Tara, Central Park and Yavana's Pace all boasted Group 1 form, whilst Travelmate had acquitted himself with great credit in finishing second in two of Britain's best staying handicaps, the Northumberland Plate and the Ebor. Against this background, it beggars belief that anyone at Portman Square might have been prepared to turn a blind eye to the Rule book when there was a very good chance that a banned Ray Cochrane might fuel the fire of Australian resentment.

Whilst press attention naturally centred around Godolphin's problems with Kayf Tara and the Cochrane affair, Yavana's Pace continued to enjoy a smooth preparation. Local observers noted his solid track work and Johnston pronounced himself happy with the horse's wellbeing. Despite Deirdre's view that Yavana's Pace was possibly best over one and a half miles, Mark was positive about his prospects, pointing out that despite its two-mile trip the Cup is often won by a ten-furlong horse. This was to prove strangely prophetic. Double Trigger's dismal run in 1995 still puzzles Johnston but he did come away that year feeling it was important not to be too hard on horses when they are abroad. Recalling Trigger's preparation: "I remember having Double Trigger doing something like fifteen laps around the Sandown track. This time we have been much easier on Yavana's Pace, which I think is the way to do it." Yavana's Pace's chances were further enhanced when the local stewards agreed he need not participate in the pre-race parade. It was felt that the poor showing of Yavana's Pace in the Ebor was largely due to his pre-race exertions and Racing Victoria viewed Johnston's request to excuse the horse from the parade as a safety issue. Alas, the draw did him no favours, though, as he was eventually allotted stall eighteen. If he were to win from there he would become the first horse to do so in the Cup's one hundred and thirty-nine year history. Asked how important it was to him for Yavana's Pace to run with distinction, Johnston, afraid that a poor performance might suggest that he had failed to learn from previous experiences, replied: "Let's just say it would mean a huge amount if he didn't run well."

Despite latching on to Travelmate (as low as 9/2 on the eve of the race), the Australian betting public wrote off Yavana's Pace's chances. The gelding was 25/1 on the eve of the race, a price which Mark described as "bordering on the insulting". As usual, Mark confirmed that no specific instructions would be given to Richard Hughes. He stated: "I am making a point of not saying anything to him about where he should be, particularly from his eighteen draw. I don't know what the other jockeys in the race are going to do." However, beforehand Saeed Bin Suroor confirmed that Dettori would try to cross Central Park from stall nineteen and obtain a front-running position.

Once again, a Group 1 race brought real disappointment to the Johnston camp. In what turned out to be a rough affair, Frankie Dettori dictated the pace on Central Park (sent off at 50/1). However, he did so only steadily, resulting in a number of barging matches taking place in mid-division. Shaken up two furlongs from home, it looked for a while as though Central Park would repel all challengers but, fifty metres from home, Rogan Josh foiled him with a determined, late run, thus giving trainer Bart Cummings his eleventh cup success. As for Yavana's Pace, he ran disappointingly to finish twelfth of twenty-four, just two places out of the prize money. Conscious of the need to tuck the horse in and save ground where possible Hughes repeatedly restrained the gelding through the early stages. However, every time Richard attempted to rein him back, Yavana's Pace stuck his head in the air, forfeiting ground. As far as six furlongs from home Mark recalls thinking that the horse was just too far back. In the straight he was travelling well enough but could never land a blow at the principals, finishing about eight lengths behind the winner. Incidentally, Rogan Josh had run in and won the

Louis Vuitton Mackinnon Stakes over ten furlongs just three days previously, reinforcing Johnston's view that the Cup can be won by a ten-furlong horse.

Richard Hughes confirmed that the race was both slowly run and very rough, memorably likening his experience to "riding in the Triumph Hurdle— except they go much faster in the Triumph Hurdle". He said, "I was happy with my position early on, but it was a crawl and I could never quite get back into it when they quickened. The race just wasn't run to suit him."

Mark was bitterly disappointed by his charge's failure to land a blow, so much so that in the immediate aftermath he was doubtful whether he would try again. His pessimism wasn't born out of pique at a lack of success to date but rather from a rational reconsideration of the equation between the cost of competing and its potential rewards. He told reporters: "It took me a long time to come back after Double Trigger. My reservation is simply that it is so expensive. You have to wonder whether it is sensible to stake £50,000 on a handicap. With Yavana's Pace we even had the variable of wondering whether he would get to the start." In fact, Yavana's Pace was just two places and two and a half lengths away from tenth prize of £24,000, which would have paid about half the bill incurred. Although Yavana's Pace had finished well down the field and disappointed his trainer in the process, it's arguable that his finishing position owed more to a poor draw and ill-luck in running than to any failure in preparation. This did not make the bitter pill of disappointment any easier for him to swallow in the immediate aftermath.

Whilst reflecting on the race Mark could not resist having a swipe at Colin Alderson's intemperate remarks. "They say our horses are B grade", he observed, "but they give them plenty of weight. It's interesting that three of the first five home were Australian horses with low weights." Thus, Kingsley House's Group 1 target remained outstanding. Could Fruits of Love triumph in Tokyo?—time would tell.

November had started quietly, low-key meetings at Nottingham, Redcar and Catterick on the first two days of the month failing to produce a winner. An eventful fixture at Musselburgh on the 3rd produced two but, regrettably, a two-year-old called Faraj broke a leg entering the straight and had to be destroyed. He was one of two fatalities at the seaside track on the day. The winners were Virgin Soldier, following up his Lingfield success and, appropriately enough, Littlepacepaddocks, a two-year-old sister to none other than Yavana's Pace.

The tragic death of Faraj and John Berry's Warring Kingdom at Musselburgh served only as a starter to an unpalatable main course of misery for Middleham generally. On November 5th Mark was sitting in his car on the moor reading the *Racing Post* and waiting for the string to arrive for exercise when he noticed a horse fall awkwardly at one of the adjacent schooling fences. From the reaction of those on the scene he suspected immediately that it was French Holly, winner of the 1998 Royal & SunAlliance Hurdle at the Cheltenham Festival. He'd just begun his career over fences and was being aimed at the Cheltenham Gold Cup. Regrettably, those suspicions were well founded. Regular pilot Andrew Thornton had travelled north for a routine schooling session and at the last of a second spin over the fences the massive eight-year-old had brushed through the top, for some reason failing to get his landing gear down, and landed on his neck. Mark raced to the stricken horse only to find that his neck was broken and that he'd died more or less instantly. French Holly, known as a gentle giant by his trainer, Ferdy Murphy, had promised to bring Middleham success at a level not enjoyed under National Hunt Rules since the days of Neville Crump. His loss came as a body blow to Middleham's racing community, not least to his devoted lass, Lissette George. The contrast between French Holly's fatal accident and the calamity which had befallen Fruits of Love earlier in the year could hardly have been more striking. Here was a horse going through routine exercise in an environment in which he would have been perfectly settled. Yet he was snuffed out as quickly as any candle. The drama in which Fruits of Love became embroiled couldn't have unfolded more slowly. No situation could have been more artificial and stressful for a horse—yet he survived. Sadly, racing folk require to come to terms with this type of tragedy all too often. Not for the first time, Alastair Down found *les mots justes* when writing in the *Post*: "One more dead gelding does not carry much weight in the scales of calamity world wide, but this is racing's loss, our business, a parish matter. It is painful because it is close to home and we understand what it means. Above all we know all too well what it is we no longer have the chance to see. It's a sad sunset that comes just halfway through the day."

On November 6th, the final day of the turf season, Johnston was three-handed in the November Handicap, Akbar, Murghem and Robin Lane all having their supporters. However on this occasion the spoils went to another Middleham trainer, Chris Thornton, whose brave filly Flossy prevailed by a head, in the process providing a little compensation for the village's great loss. A win by one of the Johnston trio would have taken British win and place prize money past the £1 million mark. As it was, the running total at the end of the day's racing stood at £986,000.

The following day in Germany, Joe Fanning partnered Spirit of Love in a listed race at Mulheim over seventeen furlongs. A facile success resulted, rekindling hopes of a return to peak form in 2000 for the horse who had promised so much when romping away with the Cesarewitch thirteen months earlier.

The Virgin Soldier bandwagon rolled on, the gelding completing a treble at Lingfield on November 8th, and the David Abell show continued back at the Surrey course on the 11th when Alberich prevailed in a hot conditions stakes. Twenty-four hours later stable amateur Carol Williams enjoyed an armchair ride on Virgin Soldier at Southwell, a race notable in that it provided a debut victory for the gelding on fibresand and also resulted in Carol losing her claim, this being her eleventh success.

On the other side of the world Yavana's Pace returned to action. The gelding had remained in Australia after the Melbourne Cup until it became clear whether he would be invited to run in the Hong Kong International Vase, for which he was a reserve. Thus, in an effort to recoup part of the £50,000 which had been laid out on his Melbourne Cup bid, it was decided to run him in the Grade 2 Sandown Classic over one and a half miles, worth £130,000 to the winner.

Yavana's Pace had nicked the inside of his right fore at Flemington and was a bit sore afterwards; however a full recovery had been made and the VRC's Greg Nichols suggested to Mark that the Sandown race might provide a suitable opportunity for the gelding. Acutely aware of the costs already incurred, Mark decided to minimise further expense by staying at home. Richard Hughes was again available and flew into Australia just fourteen hours beforehand. With there being no sign of anyone else willing to go on, he took Yvanna's Pace straight into the lead. This wasn't the gelding's preferred style of running but at least, as Mark later remarked, you can't complain about the pace if you make it yourself. In a blanket finish Yavana's Pace was just run out of things, finishing sixth, just one and three quarter lengths behind the winner, the New Zealand horse Aerosmith, and missing out on prize money by a short head. Ironically, this time Yavana's Pace finished just in front of the Melbourne Cup winner, Rogan Josh!

Despite missing out, this was a good run from Yavana's Pace. Richard Hughes commented afterwards: "the going may have been a bit hard for him. He has a high galloping action and likes to be able to jab the ground. He kept fighting on and was coming back at them at the finish."

Yavana's Pace didn't make the line up for the Hong Kong race and travel problems associated with the carriers, Cathay Pacific, losing slots at Heathrow led to the gelding eventually being flown back to Stansted Airport on November 17th. After such a frustrating and expensive Australian adventure, the Keaneys might have been expected to have been soured by the whole experience.

However, in spite of a round trip of 24,000 miles, a couple of near misses and an approximate outlay of £50,000 John Keaney was upbeat. "Yavana's Pace really did us proud" he commented. "It was certainly a long way to send him to Australia, but it couldn't have been done any more professionally than the way Mark and his staff did the job, and the fact that we haven't got anything to show for the venture is just unfortunate." He confirmed that the plan was for the gelding to winter at home in Ireland before returning to Kingsley House next season. "I don't have any specific target in mind, but I'm sure Mark will again pull something out of the hat" he added. It will be interesting to see how the gelding is campaigned by Johnston in the season to come, given his plethora of riches in the stayers' department.

Despite having been raised 10 lb in the ratings, Virgin Soldier made it five in a row at Wolverhampton on November 17th, Joe Fanning able to ease down well before the line. This was rather a special win for the stable as it brought up the million. Goal number two in the bag, with almost a month and a half to spare! The David Abell-owned contingent had certainly excelled them-selves in recent weeks.

Abell was himself ecstatic when Virgin Soldier took his tally to six at Southwell on the 22nd. Although fortunate enough to own numerous prolific winners down the years he had never before had a horse complete a sequence of six straight wins. "Vindaloo won eleven in a season, Star Rage won nine one year and five another, Branston Abby won six and two fives and Jimmy the Skunk won six, but none of them ever managed to win six on the bounce," he enthused. Despite Michael Hills easing the gelding once clear, the winning distances on this occasion were five lengths and sixteen lengths, the third horse Legal Lunch providing a solid yardstick with which to gauge Virgin Soldier's recent striking improvement. At Lingfield on November 8th, in the third of that sequence, he'd received 22 lb from Legal Lunch and given him a two-and-three-quarter-length beating. At Southwell, he was receiving only 5 lb but beat Peter Harris' horse by twenty-one lengths!

All good things come to an end and Virgin Soldier's enchanted run of success duly did so at Lingfield on November 26th. In retrospect it was always likely that he would find twelve furlongs on the sharp side, eventually finishing like a train but failing by a head to peg back the ultra-game Noukari. Nonetheless, Virgin Soldier and Kayo are both excellent examples of Johnston's ability to improve horses that have been in training elsewhere. Perhaps the best example in that respect is Yavana's Pace, who joined him as a six-year-old, having not won a race since his first start in Ireland at four.

Late-season foreign assignments were now being tackled by a number of Kingsley House stars. Lord Hartington's Awake, so impressive when trouncing a large field in soft ground at Newbury, was despatched to Maisons-Laffitte on November 22nd to contest the Prix Zeddaan (Listed) over six furlongs. Two furlongs out the Middleham raider held a command-ing advantage over the field. However, Awake began to roll under pressure and, hanging left, hampered Criquette Head's Tencarola, upon whom Olivier Doleuze was unable to ride a proper finish. Awake battled on to take second behind the fast-finishing Zeiting, but the stewards eventually placed him fourth behind the hampered horse. Joe Fanning, who received a four-day ban for his ride recalled: "He got bored in front and that's why he wandered. He went on again when company arrived!"

One week later, at the same course, Robin Lane was on a mission to achieve a Listed success which would enhance her value as a potential broodmare. The Prix Belle de Nuit, restricted to fillies and mares, seemed an ideal target, but she disappointed, weakening after setting a good pace to the home turn. She'd proved a gallant servant and deserved a more fitting swansong, her next appointment being a union at stud with the 1998 St James's Palace Stakes winner Dr Fong—perhaps someone had told her!

A trio of French raids was completed on November 30th when Sinon contested the Prix Denisy (Listed) over fifteen furlongs at Saint-Cloud on heavy ground. Fanning was able to capitalise on the considerate reintroduction to racing given to him by Darryll Holland in the Cesarewitch and, relishing the going, Sinon registered a facile success. Johnston had been the epitome of patience with the colt and took particular pleasure in seeing him recapture form. A bright future for this lightly-raced horse looks assured, especially granted similarly testing conditions in 2000.

The main focus of attention for the stable at the end of November was the nineteenth running of the Japan Cup (Group 1) at Fuchu, Tokyo, the penultimate leg of the Emirates World Series and a race which has been kind to European challengers over the last few years, its winners including Lando, Singspiel and Pilsudski. Fruits of Love was aiming to atone for his Canadian near miss and with the ground likely to be in his favour there was good reason to hope that that elusive Group 1 victory might yet materialise. His preparation for the race, however, was punctuated by what Johnston described as "various niggles". Filling in a leg denied him the opportunity of giving the Hansel colt one more gallop before shipping him abroad, and though that seemed fine when Fruits of Love left Middleham on November 17th his weight was some 5 kg or so higher than ideal. On arrival in Japan his supply of hay was confiscated and alternative local supplies provided. This was a further hindrance, especially in the lead-up to a big race. The rigours of international travel place enough of a strain upon thoroughbreds; to further disrupt their normal eating/sleeping habits just adds to their problems.

Amazingly, given the high-tech profile of Japanese society, communications between Robynne and the stable were difficult. The staff had no access to the internet or even to a basic fax machine. Johnston's staff had no option other than to rely on public telephones and found the cost of telephone cards to be ludicrously expensive. This was surprising considering the Japan Racing Association had been generous enough to meet the costs associated with running Fruits of Love and to pay for the travelling expenses incurred by Mark, Deirdre, and Mick Doyle.

The Japan Cup is another special event in the international sporting calendar. A crowd of 150,000 watch the race, the tenth on an eleven-race card; prize money is phenomenal, second only to the Dubai World Cup (this year's winner collected £1,071,545 and even the owners of the fifth horse received more than £105,000) and there is a genuine, widespread enthusiasm among the crowd for racing as a sport, not just as a punting medium. Furthermore, (BHB take note) racing is regarded as a hobby for the "young and hip".

Jockey plans altered dramatically when Kieren Fallon, Fruity's intended partner, incurred a three-day ban for careless riding at Sha Tin on November 21st . Johnston's first-choice deputy was Michael Hills, as he had ridden the horse in the Princess of Wales's Stakes. Hills readily agreed to ride, but when it became clear that his visa application would not be processed in time Johnston was happy to turn to South African Michael Roberts, then based in Tokyo on a three-month licence. Roberts had won the 1995 running on the German-trained horse Lando. "I'm very happy to have Michael. He is very professional and has ridden a lot of winners for me over the years" commented Mark to Rodney Masters of the *Racing Post*.

Coral opened a book on the race on November 23rd, installing Fruits of Love at 6/1 third favourite behind the Prix du Jockey-Club, Irish Derby and Prix de l'Arc de Triomphe winner, Montjeu and leading Japanese hope, Special Week. The following day Fruits of Love was brought from the special quarantine area to Fuchu Racecourse, to enable Deirdre partner him at exercise until the big day. Such is the enthusiasm of the Tokyo public for racing that when the foreign challengers arrived to tune up at 6.45 am on Thursday the 25th, they were met by around 2,600 fans and more than 70 cameramen. Each piece of work was timed and shown live on a giant screen. Deirdre cantered Fruits of Love once around the turf track and let him jog for two furlongs or so. Things seemed well; all that remained was to keep everything crossed!

Montjeu and Fruity apart, the international challenge for the race comprised Indigenous from Hong Kong, the 1998 Epsom Derby winner High-Rise (the mount of Frankie Dettori) top German horse Tiger Hill, winner of the Grosser Preis von Baden (itself to be included in Phase II of the World Series roster) and fifth in the Arc, Borgia, fresh from a highly promising but unlucky run in the Breeders' Cup; and dual Champion Stakes winner, Alborada. Regrettably, the last named had to be withdrawn after sustaining a heel injury, denying George Duffield an opportunity to shine in Tokyo. Michael Roberts was dismissive of the home team for the race. "I think this is probably the weakest team that Japan has ever had in the race" he commented. "The best horse, Special Week, won the Emperor's Cup last time out but I couldn't get too excited about his chance."

All looked set fair for Fruits of Love's challenge, especially as he had the firm ground he required. Conversely, doubts over Montjeu's ability to handle the conditions were growing. Yet, on course, Fruits of Love was allowed to start at odds of nearly 20/1. Sadly, they proved realistic as he failed to sparkle, finishing ninth behind Special Week who gave star Japanese jockey Yutaka Take his first victory in the race. Indigenous took second and High-Rise signalled a return to his best form, finishing third, three quarters of a length ahead of Montjeu. Reviewing the race later that week and noting the travelling difficulties and unsuitably firm going encountered by John Hammond's great horse, Tony Morris summed up Montjeu's Japan Cup experience when he said: "The curious decision to run him never looked like being vindicated as the race developed".

Whilst racegoers chanted Take's name as Special Week was led back to the winner's enclosure, Johnston, Roberts and Doyle were holding an inquest. Fruits of Love had raced in mid division, come off the final bend in fourth and then, slightly squeezed for racing room by High-Rise, failed to pick up. Pressed for comments by an army of reporters, Johnston and Roberts offered no excuses. Privately, though, Roberts wondered whether the run was due to temperament on the horse's part. What puzzled Johnston in particular was that instead of running on, as he had in all his other races this year, Fruits of Love had flattened out tamely.

The realisation that Group 1 success had eluded him for the year lay heavily on Mark's shoulders. He began a period of even more intense reflection on his operation—but more of that later!

Notwithstanding the disappointments arising from Tokyo, November was generally a satisfactory month for the stable. Its haul of 9 winners was above average at this stage of the season and indeed had been bettered only in 1996. The running total for the year was now 112, achieved at a monthly strike rate of 13.2%, moving the yearly strike rate figure to 15.1%. Win prize money in Britain now stood at £665,444, whilst the foreign total moved on by £20,003, thanks to Spirit of Love and Sinon.

CHAPTER SIXTEEN

December 1999

F lat racing in Britain at this time of year is restricted to the all-weather circuits of Lingfield, Southwell and Wolverhampton. As the month began, Mark came to the conclusion that, even though he is leading trainer on the all-weather over the last five years and remains committed to the principle of racing on sand, the number of runners he was likely to send out this winter would be severely depleted. There were three main reasons for this. Firstly, some of his major owners had expressed the desire that their horses should not be asked to run on equitrack or fibresand. Secondly, in Mark's own view, there were concerns about the maintenance of all-weather tracks and the nature and extent of injuries sustained by his horses. Lastly, the 1999 turf campaign had resulted in a considerable number of Kingsley House horses being rated by the official handicappers at 90 or above. At that level Johnston reckoned there was no incentive to keep horses on the boil. Opportunities are severely limited and prize money not high enough to justify a winter campaign with the attendant risk of injury.

In fairness to Arena Leisure, who own the three British all-weather tracks, they are aware of the need to increase prize money and are trying to address the problem. They recently proposed to boost racing in January and February by injecting an extra £100,000 into prize money within that period. The proposal required the backing of the British Horseracing Board for a request to increase the basic daily rate of prize money from the Levy Board. Disappointingly, the BHB declined to support these proposals in full. So by the time Fruits of Love was due to contest the Hong Kong Vase on December 12th only three domestic runners had been sent out, Netta Rufina being closest to success when second over two miles at Wolverhampton on the first day of the month.

Before leaving for Hong Kong, Mark had attended the Horserace Writers and Photographers Association lunch at the Royal Lancaster Hotel, London on December 6th. There, he was delighted to accept the Stable Staff of the Year award (the d'Avigdor Goldsmid Trophy) on behalf of Robynne Watton, who was already in Hong Kong supervising Fruits of Love.

Once in Hong Kong, Mark reflected further upon the horse's puzzling performance in Tokyo. Before arriving there, he'd decided that his failure to pick up might have resulted from his being ridden closer to the pace than usual. Thus, Johnston was happy for Kieren Fallon to revert to his original style of riding the horse from off the pace. The *Racing Post* picked up on these reflections with the headline: "Fruits to Play Waiting Game". Little were they to know just how long a waiting game this would prove to be. After Fruits of Love had cantered on the Sha Tin track the Saturday before the race, Mark, noticing some apparent abnormalities, ordered a scan of the colt's left fore-leg. This revealed minor damage to the suspensory ligament and following much discussion with Mick Doyle it was decided not to put the horse's career in jeopardy by running him. "I would imagine he did it in Japan, which would explain why he ran a bit flat there" commented Mark. In a way, some reassurance was gleaned from the likelihood that Fruits of Love's disappointing run in the Japan Cup had probably resulted from the injury. Granted a full recovery, Fruits of Love should be able to continue to compete at the highest level. However, the process of recovering from such an injury is notoriously slow and, even at this stage, Johnston began to think in terms of a return at Royal Ascot 2000.

The Vase was won by Andre Fabre's Borgia, a proven Group 1 performer, who incredibly was allowed to start at odds of 23.9/1. Luminaries such as Indigenous and Rogan Josh failed to make the frame. It was no consolation to Mick Doyle that proceedings were run at a crawl and would therefore not have suited Fruits of Love. Indeed, Doyle was so despondent in the aftermath of the injury, that he wondered whether such a globetrotting policy was the right one to have adopted. The chances of injury are maximised when horses participate at the highest level, regardless of location. They are pushed to their physiological limits, often in rough races. Each one is usually a real battle and horses are often pretty stiff and sore afterwards.

In slightly less exotic surroundings, namely Southwell on December 17th, Mel Pilkington's Sea Squirt made a brave attempt to break the stable's duck for the month, finishing second in the mile maiden. That honour fell to Ron Huggins' Double Banger, a two year old colt by Ela Mana Mou, who ran out a facile winner of a ten furlong maiden at Lingfield twenty-four hours later. Indeed, Double Banger proved to be Johnston's last winner of the century, only a handful of runners being sent out before the dawn of the new millenium. Not that this should be interpreted as a sign of inactivity! Even then Mark and his staff were hard at work keeping the older horses ticking over and taking those annual early steps along the road to turning ugly duckling yearlings into next year's swans. Even over Christmas approximately half his staff were working. On Christmas Day itself the week's runners, Glenwhargen and Ambushed, went out at 8 am. Fruits of Love swam and then went on the horse walker; the other horses were mucked out in their boxes and fed. The staff worked from 8 am for just over an hour and again from 4.30 pm until 6 pm. Attention to detail demanded nothing less!

Lest it be thought that the trainer expects more from his staff than he demands of himself Johnston, it should be noted, works seven days a week, year in, year out and rarely treats himself to a holiday. It occurred to me in December that he had not had a break with his family and I asked him when he planned to relax! He hoped that the family might manage one in February, though as their intended destination is Dubai, racing matters will no doubt still be on his mind!

December's return of one winner from eleven runners gave a monthly strike rate of 9.1%. The final strike rate for the year stood at a highly respectable 15%. Win/place prize money in Britain totalled £1,008,193 and, with the addition of foreign earnings, the final tally of prize money was £1,521,687.93. Races won in Britain totalled a hundred and thirteen, supplemented by eight successes abroad.

When meeting Mark two days before Christmas I found him in reflective mood, pondering a disappointment which I imagined may have preoccupied him since Tokyo. As we watched work on the Low Moor, a biting wind making this slice of North Yorkshire feel as exposed as a North Sea oil platform, he bemoaned the fact that, for all that the season had been particularly successful in terms of races won and the amount of prize money earned, the failure to achieve a Group 1 success underlined a crucial task facing MJRL as it entered the new year—that of attracting better quality raw material. I asked again whether being based in Middleham was a negative factor in the eyes of potential customers. However, Johnston would not hear of this. We spoke also of the difficulty in persuading owners to invest in better quality yearlings. The reality is, however, that to compete for those whose pedigrees stamp them as horses with Group 1 potential requires a financial standing which transcends the wealth of lottery winners. What's more, even if a trainer is lucky enough to enjoy the patronage of someone with that clout, there are no guarantees that the myriad pitfalls which prevent potential being realised can be avoided.

Nonetheless, Johnston has already demonstrated time and again the ability to coax maximum achievement from raw material at the lower end of the market. What he now relishes most of all is the opportunity to handle yearlings of the highest class. We discussed a *Racing Post* article from early October which seemed to illustrate the nature of his predicament. It featured the Newmarket Houghton Yearling Sales-topper, a Fairy King colt sold for 1,700,000 gns to the powerful John Magnier/Michael Tabor team. The vendors had been Ballygallon Stud, the County Kilkenny-based breeding operation of Roy and Belinda Strudwick, breeders of Double Trigger and Double Eclipse. Mark was delighted that the Strudwicks had enjoyed such success but, in a perfect world, would have loved to train the colt himself. Alternatively, he would have liked to have been able to bid for him or, for that matter, any of the top ten lots sold. Realistically, the best outcome that Mark might expect arising from the Strudwick's good fortune was that they might now keep a horse in training which would otherwise have been destined for the sales. My mind went back to Catterick on June 30th and to the race that Mrs Strudwick's Netta Rufina had lost when slipping coming out of the stalls. The plan that day had been to win another race purely to enhance his value at the forthcoming July Sales. Mark had been genuinely disappointed when that had come unstuck; I had been party to the end of his telephone conversation with Belinda Strudwick afterwards. To him, the need to tell the owner about the outcome of a run-of-the-mill handicap is every bit as pressing as the need to report to the owner of a Group 1 horse.

Given the fairly downbeat tone of our conversation on the moor I was delighted to read Mark's contribution to the *Racing Post* feature entitled "The Shape of Things to Come" published on January 3rd 2000. In conveying his predictions on what the next decade might hold for British racing, I was reassured to note that he hadn't lost his sense of humour ; suggesting that by 2010 Henry Cecil will have taken early retirement from training to allow him to become one of our premier owner-breeders, with his string being trained in Middleham, North Yorkshire (God's own country). Rather a nice idea, don't you think?

CHAPTER SEVENTEEN

Review of the Season

The goals set by Johnston at the start of 1999 proved challenging enough. There were times throughout the year, April and early May spring to mind, when a target of one hundred winners in Britain seemed far from certain to be achieved. Some horses were not running well; others looked badly out of condition. Johnston was concerned that the feeding regime (or perhaps a failure by the staff to ensure proper implementation of the regime) was not producing the results he expected; injuries were taking longer to clear, and the staff as a whole were not responding effectively to the challenges which these problems posed. At one point during the season the number of sick or lame horses within the stable totalled 78! Thankfully, largely through his own attention to detail and his unwillingness to tolerate anything other than the highest standards of stable management and horse husbandry, these problems were resolved and, as the condition of the horses improved, so too did results. In the end, the century was achieved comfortably enough. Kayo's win at Newcastle on October 20th provided the one hundredth domestic success, comfortably before Doncaster's curtain call. In 1998, end-of-season wins on the all-weather had been required to top the winning total up to a ton.

Johnston was naturally delighted at having achieved this target for a sixth year in succession. However, might it be argued that single-minded pursuit of personal goals cuts across the idea of putting the owners' interests first? In other words, was it sometimes tempting to run a horse in the hope of victory when cool, calm reflection might have suggested that the right thing was to leave him at home? No, according to Mark. Johnston's ideal racehorse is one who feeds well, works hard, retains its condition and flourishes on racing. Owners who patronise the stable know this from the outset and presumably share his view that racehorses are for racing. The horses are run on their merits in the class of race appropriate to their ability. Horses aren't dropped in class simply to notch up another winner for MJRL.

Although happy with results, Mark had not forgotten the extent of his concerns when things were not going so well earlier in the year. He had resolved then to make changes and on the first morning of the York Ebor meeting outlined to me a major reorganisational plan.

Johnston's fierce intensity and desire to succeed can spill over into moodiness and anger. He finds it difficult to accept that staff will not (or cannot) invest as much time, effort and thought in resolving problems as he is prepared to. This produces a level of frustration in him which, on occasions, surfaces at weekly management meetings. From my limited observation of these I would say that his agitation is counter-productive in that some, though not all, staff members are perhaps even less likely to take personal responsibility for their decisions and actions, preferring to adopt a stance of collective responsibility (or more realistically collective anonymity). Johnston is aware of this danger and perhaps recognises that it is something of a failing on his part that the weekly meetings all too rarely involve a full and frank exchange of views on controversial matters.

Mark finds staff management the most stressful and difficult part of the business and, consequently, has invested much thought and energy in working out how to better motivate senior staff whose skills he respects but whose personal or emotional stake in every aspect of the business he feels should be increased. Some within the industry misread his passion and intensity as abrasiveness or arrogance; indeed it has been suggested to me that the stable motto "always trying" is to some people a reflection of Mark's own personality! Certainly he is a man of strongly held views who is not afraid to articulate them to any audience in plain terms. However, in my experience, those views are genuinely held, reached only after careful thought and, more often than not, founded on a sense of what is right for horse-racing in general. Mark enjoys the opportunity to debate his views and as Mick Doyle has pointed out: "with Mark you can speak your mind over a jar, and he doesn't hold back either. But if he disagrees with you, he doesn't disown you the following morning."

Whilst returning from work on August 17th, Mark set out for me the master plan he had designed to increase the personal stake of the management team in the fortunes of the business. He had decided that the current "vertical" management structure of trainer/assistant/head lad/second head lads should disappear to be replaced by an entirely new approach. At the end of the season, boxes in the Kingsley House and Warwick House yards would be divided into five modules; each module would consist of thirty boxes which, in turn, would come under the control of a head lad; those head lads would have responsibility for every aspect of the care, management and performance of the horses in their module; staff would be chosen by each head lad on a basis similar to the "draft pick" used in American football; thus staff wishing to move to another module within the stable would require to negotiate transfer terms, etc. Obviously, all these functions would be subject to Mark's overriding supervision.

As we discussed the pros and cons Mark stopped the car outside a field in which a herd of cattle was grazing quietly. He told me that these were his (as close to a hobby as it gets for MJ) and that Susanna had reported one of the calves sick. We were going to walk round the field, find the calf in question and check out what was wrong. As he opened the gate Mark casually pointed out to me "oh, I should tell you there's a bull in this field but you should be as safe as you can ever be when there's a bull around". Thankful that I was not wearing red, I trudged warily around the field, lagging slightly behind Mark so that I could discreetly keep a weather eye open for the bull, whilst also assessing the lowest part of the boundary wall to make for if the worst came to the worst. I suspect Mark realised my thoughts were else-where!

I couldn't help wondering how the new structure would impact upon the individuals most closely concerned with the management of the business. How for example would Brendan Holland, the current head lad, be treated under this scheme? Mark explained that Brendan would be offered a posi-tion as one of the head lads, as would Jock Bennett and Debbie Kettlewell. He proposed to promote another of the more experienced lads or lasses to that position and to advertise for a new member of staff to fill the other vacancy, partly to freshen up the existing team and partly to stimulate new methods and to enhance the aspect of friendly rivalry between the five new modules. Robynne Watton would remain in her role as travelling head lass and Bobby Elliott's role would remain unchanged. Susanna's role would be more restricted in that, in practical terms, her work would be confined to that of resident vet. In Johnston's absence, whether racing, at the sales or abroad, the person in overall control, perhaps with a title of Head of Racing Operations, would be Debbie Albion; a reflection of the trainer's respect for Debbie's hard work, forthright attitude and her feeling for horses generally.

The point of the exercise was to give individual staff members a more compelling reason to work harder for success than pool money alone. Johnston reckoned that by encouraging individuals to give more of themselves, the overall performance of the stable would be improved. On a secondary level, the splitting of the staff pool into five units would also assist Johnston in being able to identify those responsible for certain acts, omissions or practices. For example, problems in the proper administration of the feeding regime for one module might result in their horses looking out of condition or underweight. Mark's task in assessing why this should be so would be greatly assisted. Hiding places would be harder to find.

I found it difficult to argue against the plan from an organisational point of view but, nonetheless, perceived two potential weaknesses. Firstly, I wondered how some key members of staff would react to working under the new system, especially Susanna Ballinger, the boundaries of whose difficult role would be further eroded by the additional responsibilities to be assumed by the five module leaders. Secondly, I wondered whether Mark's overall ethos of putting the owners first might be prejudiced by the fairly arbitrary division of horses among the modules. For example, if Jock Bennett's module was to excel next year, might an owner feel less well served if his colt or filly was within a module enjoying less success? I put the latter concern to Mark. His view was that the head lads would not be responsible for setting standards, but simply for implementing those laid down by him, standards which would ensure that owners' interests remained central to the organisation. He will still decide what the horses eat, who will ride them, what work they will do and in which races they will run. In any event owners are not normally consulted in matters affecting the internal organisation of the stable. Initially, however, this will mean that the new structure will have to be monitored closely by Mark and he is well aware of this new facet of his own role.

In the event, prior to implementation of the new plan, Debbie Kettlewell indicated to Mark that for personal reasons she wished to broaden her horizons and left at the end of October, hoping to spend some time working in America. Around the same time Mark agreed with Susanna Ballinger that she would not form part of the revised team. Thus, when the master plan was floated, advertisements were placed for head lads plural. Mark also now required to find a resident vet.

On December 23rd Mark confirmed to me that the five head lads had been selected as follows:- Brendan Holland, Jock Bennett, Duncan Cooney, formerly head lad to Lambourn trainer Bryan Smart, Zoe Ewart and Sarah MacLean, the latter pair being drafted from within the organisation.

Andy Oliver, boasting ten years experience, had also been engaged in the role of resident vet. Mark was delighted that Andy had agreed to join the Kingsley House team as, earlier in the year, he had asked Andy to accompany him to the Keeneland sales to assist in the onerous task of examining horses and perusing endless x-rays, etc. He had been much impressed by his work. Mark was pleased with the team and really looking forward to the implementation of his new structure. Given the right leaders, he hopes that a daily awareness of the need to match the hard work and dedication of rival staff members will become apparent to every employee.

The goal of attaining £1,000,000 in prize money in Britain alone proved a tough nut for Johnston to crack in 1999. Around the beginning of September, he had expressed some reservations whether it was likely to be achieved. Yet the winners kept ticking over and that late-season purple patch with Virgin Soldier hastened the arrival of the golden moment when the barrier was smashed. Despite a paucity of runners in the final weeks, the British prize-money total ended at £1,008,193. Foriegn prize money totalled over £490,000, making the stable second only to Godolphin as the top UK stable abroad. The British figure, which includes prize money for 113 winners, 102 seconds and 69 thirds, highlights two points. Firstly, that prize money in domestic racing is pitifully low and, secondly, that Johnston's season, with the exception of the older horses, notably Fruits of Love and Yavana's Pace, could fairly be described as a triumph of quantity over quality. Largely due to Fruits of Love's exploits, foreign earnings stood at almost £270,000.

The extent of the crisis regarding prize money in British racing was flagged up by an analysis of returns submitted by forty-eight member countries to the International Federation of Horseracing Authorities in Paris. Calculations were carried out to establish the prize-money recovered annually by owners expressed as a percentage of the keep and training costs laid out by them. Similar calculations made in 1996 had revealed such a calamitous situation in Britain that they were cited in the much-maligned Financial Plan drawn up by the British Horseracing Board as the central plank of their campaign to attract a significantly higher level of Government funding into the racing industry. It would be something of an understatement to say that the plan had received a mixed reception, but if it achieved nothing else it did prompt Lord Wakeham to resign as Chairman of the BHB!

The latest analysis revealed that Britain's position had declined still further from 1996, when a return to owners of 24% ranked it just 35th out of 40 countries. Of the 48 countries in respect of whom calculations had been made, Britain was now rated joint 42nd with Ireland; owners here could now expect to recover just 22% of their outlay in prize-money. A particularly alarming aspect of the survey was that this was not a table in terms of which the total range of results was narrow. Although situated just ten places above Britain in 32nd position, Canada's percentage return to owners was 43%, almost double the British figure. Climb another nine places to 23rd and the French percentage figure was 53%-almost profligate by comparison with ours! Standing in twelfth place came Hong Kong, whose racing returned 100% to owners; at seven, the UAE 132%, and at the top of the chart Argentina, for all its financial problems of recent times, a barely credible figure of 400%.

Given these kind of statistics, was it any wonder that Sheikh Mohammed, following up the veiled warnings of withdrawal from the British racing scene contained in his landmark Gimcrack speech and the establishment of David Loder at Evry, subsequently announced the setting-up of a United States-based operation under Eoin Harty? The increasing internation-alisation of racing seems to be welcomed on all sides; indeed a more enthusiastic proponent of the idea than Johnston would be hard to find. But do our politicians grasp the basic fact that such internationalisation will only marginalise our racing industry still further, thereby reducing its net contribution to the Exchequer, unless it is given the support necessary to allow it to withstand such developments?

The third goal set by Mark at the outset of the year was to achieve a Group 1 success. Despite the best efforts of Fruits of Love and Yavana's Pace this proved elusive. As we enter the twenty first century the racing and breeding industries place much value on achievements defined by results on the track, yet paper results often do not tell the whole story. No-one is more aware than Mark that Fruits of Love's failure to capture a Group 1 race to date in his career effectively restricts his stud value. Yet to adopt such a narrow interpretation of the horse's record is to fail to appreciate the extent of the achievements represented by the horse's thrilling Dubai success and his subsequent rescue, recovery and rehabilitation from that calamitous horse-box accident. That he is racing at all is remarkable; that he is racing at such a high level borders on the miraculous. The line between success and failure at Group 1 level is very thin indeed. Incidentally, one happy postscript to Fruits of Love's campaign was added when Sarah Freeman was named the "Lanson Lady of the Year" for her contribution to the racing industry, a fitting reward for her bravery, composure and skill in dealing with the stricken horse. In accepting the award, and indeed when appearing on Channel 4 Racing's *The Morning Line*, Sarah was extremely modest about her own efforts, choosing instead to pay tribute to the Fire Brigade, Robynne Watton, Gail Alderson and Fruits of Love himself.

Whilst disappointed by the failure to secure the hat-trick of pre-determined goals, Johnston can console himself by reflecting on the fact that the stable secured more wins in 1999 than in the previous season. Indeed, over the period from 1995 to 1999, Johnston's stable leads the way in Britain in terms of races won, with 565 successes, 16 more than Richard Hannon and 21 ahead of John Dunlop. In the inaugural year of the Emirates World Series, he trained the eighth-placed horse and finished seventh in the trainers' table. Out of fifty-two two-year-olds introduced to the track no fewer than twenty four won at least once, at a strike rate of 19%. In giving increased opportunities to Joe Fanning he equipped the stable with a valuable riding asset for 2000 and beyond. Above all, he further developed his experience of world racing, something that will continue to stand his stable in good stead as the trend towards internationalisation progresses.

Mark knows too that the real key to further success at top level is for him to somehow improve the overall quality of his string. I know from our conversation on December 23rd that he is constantly reflecting on the task and have no doubts whatsoever that he will continue to do so, as well as to question himself and his methods until a solution is found. Mark Johnston is a man who will not rest in his quest for continuing improvement. Until he reaches his "perfect day" you can rest assured of one thing. He'll be trying. Always trying.

CHAPTER EIGHTEEN

Preview 2000

A s to his yard's prospects for the forthcoming season Mark is cautiously optimistic. Plans have already been made for a number of horses to challenge abroad in the early part of the year, notably in Dubai, and Johnston also has a clear idea of long-term targets for some of the stable's leading lights.

His optimism is tempered by a number of factors. Firstly, there is no obvious contender for English Classic success among his three-year-olds to have raced to date. Secondly, the number of two-year-olds in the yard has been reduced from around seventy last year to fifty-five. Therefore, given the yard's usual strong performance in this department, winning opportunities are likely to be squeezed. Thirdly, the severely depleted all-weather team is most unlikely to match previous winning totals and realistically Mark anticipates that, if the number of winners for 1999 is to be equalled, a further twenty wins on turf might be required to compensate for the missed opportunities on the all weather. Likewise, late-season success for some of Mark's older handicappers has seen them rise in the weights to such an extent that his placing skills will be tested to the full.

Mark confesses that once he reaches the 100 winner mark in a season his thoughts turn to how this total can be matched or surpassed in the succeeding year. He also admits that he is already beginning to look at 2001 with a view to addressing any concerns he may already have about the forthcoming season.

The new staff structure has established itself well and already Mark is pleased by the practical and attitudinal changes which he has been able to observe.

Goals for the year have not yet been formally set, but, given the frustration associated with Fruits of Love's recent campaign, it seems reasonable to assume that Mark will be even more keen to capture a Group 1 race in 2000. Additionally, he'll surely want to repeat last year's feat of topping £1.5m in win and place prize money. Furthermore, whilst at first it might seem a trifle unambitious to aim "only" at achieving a ton of winners once more, the reduction in overall numbers and the changing profile of the stable on the all-weather circuit might well lead Mark to conclude that a target of 100 winners is plenty challenging enough.

As for the two-year-olds, Mark regards them as a "nice enough bunch" and feels that they are equally as promising as last year's crop. They include Mark's most expensive yearling purchase at 85,000gns, a half-brother to Branston Abby by Cadeaux Genereux. It is too early either to pick out potential stars or to form an opinion as to when the earliest of the two-year-olds will be ready to run. The fact that the Cadeaux Genereux colt is the most expensive yearling ever purchased by Mark highlights the quality issue with which he has to deal. The yards of those trainers he regards as his direct competitors (Messrs Cecil, Stoute, Dunlop, Gosden, Hills, and Cumani) are full of equine blue bloods, many of which have been purchased at considerably higher prices. Yet Mark has demonstrated time and again his ability to achieve success at the highest level even with comparatively cheaply bought horses, and if this year's intake proves to be as capable as last year's crop he will be well satisfied.

The three-year-old division is full of promise. Much to Mark's frustration, the stable was often not able to contest major sprints in 1999. However, this year a formidable Kingsley House team can be deployed; Fez, Awake, Eastways, Kashra and Footprints are all expected to more than hold their own and may well prove capable of winning Group races.

The yard's highest rated two-year-old in 1999 was Dramatic Quest, allotted a mark of 105 in the International Classifications. The Zafonic colt had scored at Pontefract and Ascot before running creditably against top opposition in the Group 2 Champagne Stakes at Doncaster. Although relatively exposed, hopes are high that he will make into a decent colt.

Rated 4 lb below Dramatic Quest is Jaber Abdullah's filly, Hiddnah. Her Hamilton conqueror Sarafan ended the season on a mark of 112. Mark feels that she has the scope to develop into an Oaks type and, at this early stage, is being targeted at the Italian equivalent at Milan towards the end of May.

Paradise Garden is being aimed at the inaugural running of the UAE Derby in Dubai towards the end of March and another three-year-old holding Classic entries is Littlepacepaddocks, the sister of Yavana's Pace. This filly was so weak throughout last year that Mark and owner John Keaney were in two minds whether to run her. Whilst in Australia for the Melbourne Cup, they took the decision to give her an outing at Musselburgh and were pleasantly surprised when she prevailed. There's little doubt she has considerable potential for improvement. Incidentally, those who would rubbish her chances of success at the highest level on the basis that she has "only" won at Musselburgh would do well to remember that Luca Cumani chose the seaside course to introduce his crack filly Only Royale in 1992.

Amongst his less exposed three-year-olds, two to watch out for are Hidden Brave and Robandela. The former ran once at Nottingham in October with credit and "could be anything". Mark was very sweet on the Kingmambo colt, Robandela, last year and bitterly disappointed when he finished last but one on his sole outing in a York maiden at the beginning of September. His initial reaction was to conclude that Kieren Fallon had been too easy on the colt, though the jockey had reported that Robandela was "weak and going nowhere". However, seven days after York, Robandela was found to be lame and a fractured pelvis was subsequently diagnosed. In retrospect, it is probable that the injury occurred in the race. Robandela is now back in full work and, given that prior to this setback Mark reckoned him the most impressive of all his horses on the gallops, his reappearance is eagerly awaited.

One other three-year-old to look out for is Carousing, by Selkirk out of a half-sister to Moon Madness and thus stoutly-bred on the dam's side. Given his pedigree, two wins over seven furlongs at Lingfield and Goodwood seemed more than encouraging. However, thereafter the colt encountered some problems and was sent back to his owner, Peter Savill. Savill reported that Carousing was very coltish at home and indicated that Mark "could geld him if you like". Mark found his attitude refreshing, as the issue of gelding is always a difficult one to resolve with owners who, understandably, want to keep alive the dream of owning a horse good enough to command a sub-stantial fee at stud. For that reason, the stable's policy is to keep horses entire until the full extent of their ability has been gauged. Furthermore, Mark has not bought nor will he buy a yearling gelding at auction. Yet he has little doubt that gelding makes racehorses easier to train and thus improvement can often be expected.

Looking at the older horses in the yard, the sprint division has been boosted by the return of Tadeo, now seven. It will be interesting to see whether he can recapture his winning ways for Mark. His presence will take some of the pressure off Gaelic Storm, for whom Mark plans a similar campaign to last year. There is also a possibility that the latter will kick off his season by con-testing a new sprint race on the Dubai World Cup card.

Mark will have a strong hand in the major handicaps with the likes of Alberich, Akbar, Mardani, Kayo and Murghem to play. In particular, Mark has always thought highly of Alberich and reports him to be in fine fettle.

The sheer strength in depth of the Kingsley House staying team is striking. As well as those prolific winners Virgin Soldier and Star Rage there's also Sinon, Spirit of Love, Cardiff Arms, Etterby Park and none other than Double Eclipse, now back in training at the tender age of eight! I put it to Mark that he has something of an embarrassment of riches in this division. He pointed out that it is difficult to keep such horses fit, healthy and sound over a whole season, citing the low number of runs last season by Spirit of Love, Sinon and Etterby Park. Mark also pointed out the benefit of having such a group of potentially well-suited galloping companions and confirmed that he would not shy away from running these horses against each other if he thought it appropriate.

Plans for Spirit of Love are as before; the Sagaro/Henry II Stakes route and see where it leads. If he recovers the sparkling form which saw him lift the 1998 Cesarewitch so easily the Cup races may be within his scope. Sinon will initially be aimed at the Yorkshire Cup (where he is likely to meet Yavana's Pace), and if all goes well he will then be aimed at French races previously contested by Double Eclipse, including the Prix Vicomtesse Vigier. Double Eclipse himself will not be rushed and his training will be taken one day at a time. So far, luckily, he has remained sound and Mark hopes to reintroduce him in a conditions race at Haydock.

In late-January, The Winning Line asked Mark to resume training Happy Change and the ex-New Zealand horse, Cardiff Arms. Plans for Happy Change are fluid at present but it is perhaps a sign of Mark's regard for the horse that he sees him as a potential successor to Yavana's Pace. His progress should be watched carefully. Like Happy Change, The Winning Line initially regarded Cardiff Arms as a jumping prospect. Mark liked this gelding's work very much last year and is delighted to have him back in the team.

Peter Savill's Royal Rebel ran some good races in 1999, notably at Lingfield and Leopardstown though was just below the best of his age. Now gelded, Mark is keen to see whether he'll now progress to the highest level. Aspirations are high and his long-range target is the Irish St Leger.

Mark is especially keen to see Yavana's Pace build upon last year's successes. The gelding is now eight, unusually old for a Group 1 performer, and both Mark and the owners are very aware of the passage of time. With that in mind, he may well head for Dubai in March before also being campaigned at the Irish St Leger then, hopefully, gaining an invitation to the Hong Kong Cup meeting. Mark was a little aggrieved that the handicappers' lukewarm reaction to the gelding's wins in the March Stakes and September Stakes meant no Hong Kong invitation was received last year. There is no sign yet that age is catching up with Yavana's Pace. Joe Fanning, for one, will be hoping that the gelding continues to defy his years.

And what of Fruits of Love? At the time of writing, the results of his most recent scan suggest that the earliest feasible target is probably the Hardwicke Stakes. The Dubai World Cup meeting has already been ruled out and although the plan would also be to take in the King George VI and Queen Elizabeth Diamond Stakes once more, it may be that his season is restricted to an autumn campaign. The principal targets would then be the Canadian International and the Japan Cup. Thoughts of autumn and this horse remind me of Lord Byron's stanza:

> *"My days are in the yellow leaf*
> *the flowers and fruits of love are gone,*
> *the worm, the canker and the grief*
> *are mine alone!"*

Let us hope that there is no grief at the end of Fruits of Love's 2000 campaign and that Lord Byron simply erred in choosing the "yellow leaf" of autumn.

Instead, here's to Fruits of Love's racing days ending in the red maple leaf of the Canadian International. See you at Woodbine?

CHAPTER NINETEEN

Timeform Statistical Review

The Timeform Statistical Review provides a compendium of statistics, relating to British racing only, for hundreds of trainers and stallions, making extensive use of Timeform Ratings. Here is the entry in the latest Flat edition on Mark Johnston:-

---

M. JOHNSTON

Summary 1997-1999: Runners 289 / Winners 151 (52%)
Races won 336   Rated 100+ 36   Win prize money £2,135,095
Leading earner: YAVANA'S PACE (IRE) £133,878

Win prize money (£)	2-y-o	3-y-o	Older	All
1997	161,190	299,127	174,266	634,583
1998	127,990	455,393	256,209	839,592
1999	166,031	132,312	362,577	660,920
Cumulative	455,211	886,832	793,052	2,135,095

Winners-Horses	2-y-o	3-y-o	Older	All
1997	27-60	28-53	13-24	68-137
1998	19-42	26-62	12-24	57-128
1999	24-52	21-50	21-39	66-141
Cumulative	70-154	75-165	33-66	151-289

Wins-Runs	2-y-o	3-y-o	Older	All
1997	35-228	63-347	25-215	123-790
1998	29-170	46-279	25-164	100-613
1999	34-182	36-286	43-297	113-765
Cumulative	98-580	145-912	93-676	336-2168

Strike Rate (%)	2-y-o	3-y-o	Older	All
1997	15	18	12	16
1998	17	16	15	16
1999	19	13	14	15
Cumulative	17	16	14	15

1st(2nd) time out (%)	2-y-o	3-y-o	Older	All
1997	17(15)	9(18)	0(5)	11(14)
1998	12(12)	18(12)	13(19)	15(13)
1999	10(16)	12(23)	13(17)	11(19)
Cumulative	13(14)	13(17)	9(14)	12(16)

Profit / Loss (£1)	2-y-o	3-y-o	Older	All
1997	-37.11	-9.62	-33.87	-80.60
1998	-14.30	53.55	-4.48	34.77
1999	-48.39	-90.90	3.06	-136.23
Cumulative	-99.80	-46.97	-35.29	-182.06

Median Rating	2-y-o	3-y-o	Older	All
1997	73	78	86	77
1998	71	78	84	75
1999	77	74	90	77
Cumulative	74	76	87	76

Winners by month

	Ja	Fe	Mr	Ap	My	Ju	Jy	Au	Se	Oc	No	De
1997	9-41	10-29	9-42	4-51	14-94	13-99	21-88	19-100	11-86	4-101	7-41	2-18
1998	5-36	6-26	3-14	5-32	10-60	11-83	18-99	9-72	14-82	13-66	3-30	3-13
1999	8-29	2-21	3-25	8-63	8-102	15-109	25-103	15-75	10-85	11-98	7-44	1-11

Horses rated 100+   Akbar*, Alberich*, Atlantic Desire, Atlantic Viking, Bijou d'Inde, Cardiff Arms*, Celestial Key, Doonaree*, Double Eclipse, Double Trigger, Dramatic Quest*, Equity Princess, Fizzed, Fly To The Stars, Fruits of Love*, Gaelic Storm*, Gothenberg, Gypsy Passion, Happy Change*, Ice*, Kayo*, Land of Dreams, Lend A Hand, Mardani*, Murghem*, Naskhi, Princely Heir, Royal Rebel*, Sharp Play, Sinon*, Spirit of Love*, Tadeo, Tissifer*, Unconditional Love, White Heart*, Yavana's Pace*

* rating achieved in 1999

1999 horses rated with 'p'   Awake 97p, Carousing 94p, Champfis 66p, Cool Investment 76p, Double Banger 80p, Eastways 93p, Footprints 73p, Hidden Brave 90p, High Topper 56p, Inca Star 78p, Kind Regards 88p, Littlepacepaddocks 84p, Robandela 52p

1999 113 wins   £660,920   All Runs 113/765 (15%);
1st time 16/141 (11%); 2nd time 23/122 (19%); median rtg 77

Two-Year-Olds		**34**	**166,031**	
Aston Mara b.g	80	1	3,469	Nwc
Awake ch.c	97p	2	9,708	Eps Nwb
Bajan Belle (IRE) b.f	72	1	2,697	Crl
Break The Code (USA) b.c	81	1	3,435	Ham
Carousing b.c	94p	2	13,388	Lin Goo
Cool Investment (IRE) b.c	76p	1	3,436	Mus
Double Banger (IRE) b.c	80p	1	2,840	Lin
Dramatic Quest b.c	103+	2	11,625	Pon Asc
Eastways ch.c	93p	1	8,733	Bev
Fez ch.f	94	3	15,459	Red Don Yor
Footprints (IRE) b.f	73p	1	2,408	Red
Golden Miracle (FR) b.g	81	2	14,951	Ham Ham
Hammer And Sickle (IRE) b.c	92	2	6,044	Rip Red
Happy Diamond (USA) b.c	80+	1	4,081	Thi
Harryana b.f	79	2	9,796	Chs Red
Hiddnah (USA) ch.f	90	1	3,664	Nwc
High Cheviot b.c	82+	1	3,583	Nwc
Kashra (IRE) b.f	91+	3	27,170	Pon Goo Nmj
Kind Regards (IRE) b.f	88p	1	3,784	Bev
Linden Grace (USA) b.f	82	1	3,404	Eps
Littlepacepaddocks (IRE) b.f	84p	1	3,615	Mus
Love Lane (IRE) b.g	77	1	3,625	Bev
Paradise Garden (USA) b.c	98	1	2,253	Nwc
Splash Out (USA) b.c	78	1	2,863	Ayr

All Runs 34/182 (19%); 1st time 5/52 (10%); 2nd time 7/43 (16%); median rtg 77

Three-Year-Olds		**36**	**132,312**	
Around The World (IRE) b.f	83d	1	4,565	Pon
Atlantic Prince (IRE) b.g	86d	1	3,556	Bev
Baileys Black Tie b.g	67	2	4,918	Rip Rip
Doonaree (IRE) b.c	102	2	10,003	Nwc Cat
Evesham (USA) b.g	64	1	2,087	Cat
Forum Girl (USA) b.f	79	1	3,815	Ayr
Hormuz (IRE) b.g	89	4	15,680	Lin Lin Rip Bev
Ice b.g	100	1	7,895	Yor
Island Song (IRE) b.g	73	3	8,584	Lin Bat Flk
Kentucky Bullet (USA) b.g	69d	2	7,347	Sou Don
Lady Melbourne (IRE) b.f	76d	1	3,989	Thi
Love Blues (USA) b.g	75d	3	8,350	Wol Lin Crl
Love Diamonds (IRE) b.g	55§ a76§	1	2,710	Lin
Royal Rebel b.g	109	1	3,631	Nwc
Three Bay Trees (IRE) b.f	63	1	2,684	Lin
Tissifer b.c	114	1	10,050	Thi
Tonic b.g	89	1	3,745	Rip
Tous Les Jours (USA) b.f	70	1	2,900	Cat

Turtle b.g	54	1	2,490	Pon
Virgin Soldier (IRE) ch.g	91	6	20,093	Lin Mus Lin Sou Wol Sou
Young Sue b.f	76	1	3,220	Rip

All Runs 36/286 (13%); 1st time 6/50 (12%); 2nd time 10/44 (23%); median rtg 74

Older Horses		**43**	**362,577**	
Alberich (IRE) 4 b.g	101	2	22,220	Nwb Lin
Caerosa 4 b.f	70 a47	3	14,814	Ham Yor Bat
Darwell's Folly (USA) 4 ch.g	73§	2	5,745	Lei Wol
Etterby Park (USA) 6 b.g	89	1	8,481	Mus
Fruits of Love (USA) 4 b.c	127	1	80,050	Asc
Gaelic Storm 5 b.g	116	2	21,373	Goo Nmj
Happy Change (GER) 5 ch.h	113	1	6,522	Eps
John Bowdler Music 4 b.g	64 a73	2	4,644	Lin Sou
Kayo 4 b.g	103 a88	3	21,875	Red Nmj Nwc
Mardani (IRE) 4 b.g	102	2	15,724	Bev Yor
Netta Rufina (IRE) 4 ch.g	79	1	4,143	Mus
Rafting (IRE) 4 b.f	87	3	16,163	Mus Chs Thi
Robin Lane 4 b.f	95	1	6,382	War
Shontaine 6 b.g	56 a50	1	2,332	Ayr
Star Rage (IRE) 9 b.g	93	4	19,871	Bev Red Bev Goo
St Helensfield 4 ch.g	95	1	3,794	Nwc
Thekryaati (IRE) 4 ch.c	90	4	23,900	Lin Wol Wol Goo
Tiler (IRE) 7 br.g	89	1	3,778	Nwc
White Heart 4 b.g	114	1	13,355	Don
Windy Gulch (USA) 4 b.f	86	4	18,926	Ham Ham Nwc Nmj
Yavana's Pace (IRE) 7 ch.g	118	3	48,485	Lei Goo Eps

All Runs 43/297 (14%); 1st time 5/39 (13%); 2nd time 6/35 (17%); median rtg 90

Notable Overseas Wins		**8**	**269,725**	
Fruits of Love (USA) 4 b.c	127	1	154,652	Nad
Gaelic Storm 5 b.g	116	2	50,322	Ovl Ovl
Ice 3 b.g	100	1	5,950	Ddf
Royal Rebel 3 b.g	109	1	13,542	Leo
Sinon (IRE) 4 ch.g	111	1	13,449	Stc
Spirit of Love (USA) 4 ch.g	109	1	6,557	Mul
White Heart 4 b.g	114	1	25,253	Bad

ALWAYS TRYING

Index

C

I

J

N

O

P

T

U

V

NEW from Portway Press for 2000

A CENTURY OF CHAMPIONS
by John Randall & Tony Morris

❖ 100 makers of 20th-Century Racing

❖ Equine Hall of Fame including the worldwide Top 200

❖ Big Race Results and Records for 30 top races

❖ Human Hall of Fame, the top jockeys and trainers

All the great horses (each given a rating on the Timeform scale) are documented, along with the notable human achievements of the twentieth century.

'A BOLD AND BRILLIANT HISTORY OF THE SPORT'—*RACING POST*

'A MAGICAL HISTORY TOUR OF THE TURF'—*WEEKENDER*

'A GREAT READ ... SUPERB PHOTOGRAPHS'—*RACEFORM UPDATE*

'A CHAMPION PUBLICATION'—*DAILY TELEGRAPH*

'IRRESISTIBLE ... WRITTEN BY ACKNOWLEDGED EXPERTS'—*THE TIMES*

330 PAGES (10½"x8"), 300 photographs—£30 (plus £4 p&p)
Credit/Debit card ordering (24hrs) 01422 330540

MORE CLASSIC BOOKS FROM PORTWAY PRESS ...

'Favourite Racehorses' (368 pp hardback 9¾" x 12", published at £30) is a mighty tome, with over 400 photographs, covering the best reading from 50 years of Timeform Annuals. *The Observer* called it 'instantly addictive', the *Racing Post* labelled it 'the best racing book of the decade'. It provides a fascinating and wide-ranging insight into a golden era for racing. Enthralling from beginning to end.

'Gallant Sport' by Oxford historian John Pinfold (330 pp, hardback, published at £26) is the authentic history of Liverpool Races and the Grand National. The author's painstaking research has uncovered three more Grand Nationals (the first running was in 1836, not in 1839!). As well as rewriting racing history, this is a splendidly entertaining book with many colourful stories from Aintree's past.

'Bull' by Howard Wright (344 pp, hardback, published at £18.95) is the biography of Timeform's founder Phil Bull, who took the bookies for £4½m. As well as making a fortune out of betting—the book includes his 'golden rules' for success—Bull was a noted campaigner for reform in racing. Randall & Morris rank him the tenth most influential figure of the century in their book 'A Century of Champions'.

2a Timeform House Halifax West Yorkshire HX1 1XE
Credit/Debit card ordering (24hrs) 01422 330540